# MY HEART IS SINGING

## A Memoir

MYRNA KINSINGER FARRAJ

This story is dedicated to our grandchildren.
May you spread your wings and follow your heart.
Your grandparents love you. God loves you.

*Summer 2010*

# CONTENTS

# 1

## THE VOYAGE

When would my adventure ever begin? I was exasperated with the unexpected delays that kept coming. Our ship was anchored at Bush Docks in the New York Harbor, and for the third time, departure had been postponed to load more cargo.

At last, Agnes and I walked the plank into the massive vessel to settle into our assigned cabin and explore the deck's surroundings. As the anticipation to leave shore and start out for our destination neared, I found the event beyond exciting.

This was a unique experience for me. I was venturing out into a whole new world. It would be a lengthy journey. After sailing from New York City we'd not be setting foot on land until docking fourteen days later in Beirut, Lebanon. That wouldn't be the end of the voyage for the two of us. After arriving in Beirut we'd still need to travel by car through Syria to Amman, Jordan. *My stomach is full of butterflies! I can't wait!*

Leading up to this moment took prayerful thought on my part, but at last I decided to give up the security of going along with the urging of my college friends. They'd come up with a plan that we'd all teach in the same city and rent a house together. It was tempting to join in that course of action. The year was 1957, and I was graduating from Goshen College, a small school in Indiana. But I was restless, had a keen desire to serve, and—even more than that—longed for adventure.

This is typical me. That's the way I am. I want to do what friends are doing, but at the same time my independent spirit drives me. For now it was more than going straight from college to being a schoolteacher in Middle America. I was headed off as a volunteer with a unit of the Mennonite Central Committee, known as MCC, to teach in a girls' school in Amman for a two-year assignment. MCC is an organization that provides worldwide relief, development, and peace in the name of Christ. Agnes, also a graduate of Goshen College, would be serving in the same unit but doing relief work with Palestinian refugees in Jericho.

The *MS Slamat* was a huge Royal Rotterdam freighter with only twenty-one passengers. Mr. Hamoree, the Jordanian who'd brought his daughter to the States for heart surgery, had left her in safe hands to heal and was on his way back home to work. There were six students going to the American University of Beirut for their junior year abroad. Three young women were on their way to Lebanon to do service work, and four boys were going to Ethiopia to help build a mission. We had with us an African-American couple, both professors in Beirut universities. The Reverend Ingel, his wife, and their nine-year-old son from Lebanon, who'd spent eleven months in the States, were among our passengers.

The son was cute but spoiled and constantly bugged the guys. He longed for companions, I'm sure, and their activities attracted him. One day they got upset with his constant pestering, tied him up, put him in a box, and sat on it. *All in fun! I think?* These delightful people, along with Agnes and me, made up the paying passengers.

The ship proved pleasant and comfortable; at least the part at our disposal. Down the hall from our cabin I found the *DAMES* and further on the *BAD* and *DOUCHE*. Being rather confused while searching for the toilet, I soon learned the meaning of these words; Dutch, I assumed. There was ample room to sit in the library lounge and on the deck, with relaxing chairs everywhere. The lounge had a phonograph and a stack of current LP records. The turntable was kept busy with a variety of music, depending on the favorites of the one doing the spinning at the time. For our use on a lower deck, there was an activity room. There the most popular sport to play was Ping-Pong, a game I enjoyed and played numerous times.

For the twenty-one of us passengers there were twenty-five male Indonesians who assumed responsibility for our every need. The captain told us there were around seventy crewmen, whom we rarely saw and whom took care of the maintenance of the ship and its freight. The accessible decks for our use were high up at the front end of the massive ship, alongside the captain's and first mate's quarters. We got to know the captain as he ate with us—or should I say we ate with him? Each night we added thirty minutes to our watches to prepare us for Beirut's time zone.

At dinnertime, attractive menu cards appeared at our place settings, informing us of our anticipated meal. At first I was raving about the fabulous food. Each meal had five courses: appetizer, soup, main course, pastries, and coffee. Too soon the food became tiresome and tasteless. Along with the daily three meals, we were kept busy with teatime in the library at 10:00 a.m., 4:00 p.m., and 9:00 p.m. This helped to occupy our time, of which we had plenty. Getting used to teatime was easy, as it was a good reason to bring us together and break the monotony of the day.

Mr. Hamoree, Agnes's and my assigned table partner, had a food habit that for me was unusual, to say the least. Daily at breakfast he asked for a raw egg, which came to him in an eggcup. His ritual was to take his knife and with a quick slice, cut off the tip of the shell, throw back his head, and toss the egg down his throat, swallowing it all in one long gulp. Before long the farm girl in me began thinking, *We're almost two weeks out. These eggs can't be fresh. How can he do it?* It wasn't long until I found my morning appetite dwindling.

Two weeks turns into a lengthy time when one is limited to the space we were allotted aboard the freighter. I had with me a hefty supply of books and writing materials to keep me occupied, but knowing me, I'd soon tire of it all. In this setting where no one knew me, I hoped to be more outgoing. The truth being I was timid around new acquaintances and reluctant to open conversations or ask questions.

Not only was I shy by nature, but I'd grown up in rural Iowa where there weren't many opportunities to meet people other than those I'd known my entire life. Here was my chance to try new behaviors. I'd need to take myself in hand and reach out. *Myrna, you can do it! Everyone seems friendly. You know you're curious and want to get to know them. They won't bite. Just plunge in and start a conversation.*

Little by little I ventured to initiate chatting with my shipmates and hear about their lives and their interests. I surprised myself and found it easy and fun to make new friends, really not scary at all. The definite bonus being there was ample time to learn all about them. It was obvious no one was going anywhere.

Crossing the Atlantic was smooth going until about midway, when we passed the Rock of Gibraltar and entered the Mediterranean Sea. From then on the sea was rough. Most of the passengers got a touch of seasickness. I was one of the few lucky enough to escape that problem. One morning my stomach felt queasy, but that could be blamed on the dessert from the night before that had been laced with liquor. I vowed not to eat any more of the *Baba au Rhum* cakes. Poor Agnes felt under the weather for much of the trip.

Just as scheduled, bright and early on the morning of our fourteenth day, we spotted land out ahead. At last we could see the beautiful port of Beirut ahead on the horizon. Seeing the stone houses with their burnt-ocher roofs clinging to the mountains teased me into anticipating what was to come. *How quaint and inviting the hillsides look. I can't wait! It's so exciting!*

Disembarking took much longer than anyone had dreamed. Our ship docked far out, and it wasn't until after midday that we were transferred onto small boats and brought to shore. The sensation of walking on land after being on the moving ship for fourteen days was something I hadn't anticipated. The feeling might be similar to being inebriated, although I'd never experienced that feeling. It seemed to take forever until all our cargo was unloaded and we could go through customs. The good thing was it gave me more than ample time to regain my equilibrium and walk a straight line.

Mr. Lehman, the MCC unit director in Jordan, was waiting for Agnes and me in Beirut to help us through the tedious job of customs. We soon discovered that more items were attached to our identities than our personal belongings. The MCC had sent all sorts of supplies requested by the unit members already in Jordan at the time. It was our good fortune that Mr. Lehman was there to answer the questions posed about what we were bringing into the country, as besides our personal luggage, we had no idea what else bore our names.

Our first night off the ship was spent in an extremely hot Beirut hotel room. You could say Beirut was a city where people drove with their horns. All night long I heard one continuous discordant sound of short and long, low and high-pitched tones reverberating through our open window. It seemed that at every corner drivers laid on their horns and plowed through, hoping the honking would intimidate other drivers. The noise, coupled with the heat, didn't make for restful sleeping. After fourteen days of the soothing sound of the rolling sea, this first night in Beirut was a rude shock to my mind and body.

The following day, after going back down to the docks to collect our final baggage, we set off for our drive through Syria to Amman, Jordan. We spent a restful night in a charming guesthouse in Damascus. *Aaah! This is delightful—and peaceful, too.* Here, the scent of roses flooded our room rather than the sound of obnoxious horns. It gave me a tranquil night of sleep before the next day's drive to Amman. With abundant enthusiasm I was looking forward to what was to come. Little did I realize that I was setting out on an adventure that would change my life forever.

# 2

# LIFE IN AMMAN

WITH EAGER ANTICIPATION I arrived in Amman, Jordan, the place that was to be my home for the next couple of years. I'd seen nothing like it before. Here was a huge bustling busy city nestled in a valley with seven mountains ascending from the center. Each mountain, or *jebel* as it's known in Arabic, had its own name identifying a residential area. The Ahliyyah School for Girls, my new residence, was just off the second circle of Jebel Amman. It had been founded as an Anglican mission school known as CMS, but within the last years had become nationalized by the local church.

The delays in New York caused me to arrive late, and the school had been in session for over a week. The enrollment was more than 350 students, with all the girls wearing brown tunics with crisp white blouses. I was told there was about an equal ratio of Muslim and Christian students. Only if a girl was wearing a cross or an Allah pendant was I aware of her faith. Otherwise they all blended in as one.

The school taught prekindergarten, kindergarten, primary 1–6, and secondary I–V, the latter two of which compared to our elementary and secondary grades. Little boys attended the first three classes only and then went on to the boys' school. The school's fame was that King Hussein had been enrolled as a small lad, as were his sisters, who'd attended all the way through secondary V.

Three British women remained teaching there along with the local teachers. The board of the school seemed to want to add an American, so that's where I entered the picture. I was to reside in the school with Mary Harrison, Margaret Kidd, and Rhoda Thomas, the British teachers. We had a cook, a maid, and a gatekeeper also living within the school compound.

All the enrollees were day students from various parts of the city and arrived mainly by taxis or family drivers. It became apparent to me early on that the student body was from the elite of the city. The Ahliyyah School for Girls was considered one of the best in the country by most anyone ready to give an opinion.

To my naïve eyes, the school compound appeared inviting and attractive. The high wall around it was composed of large carved stone, as was the building with its dark green shutters and doors. Surrounding the building were attractive old pine trees. The yard was spacious with large, shapely cypress trees at the lower end with ample room left for the girls to walk, study, and play. Comfortable wooden benches were tucked in among the trees. Just inside the gate was a small stone building that housed the gatekeeper.

Daily, a vendor set up a food stand at the lower end of the compound for lunch purchases by the girls. I found their favorite was a pita loaf of falafel with lettuce, tomato, and a little *tahini* sauce. Before long it became my preferred choice as well. However, I ate lunch with Mary, Margaret, and Rhoda on the second floor of the school building and didn't often have the opportunity to eat a falafel sandwich.

My second-floor room was freshly painted a light dusty blue with a bright yellow pull curtain over the large northern window. My first impression was a favorable one. In the room I found a bed, a wardrobe, a dresser with a mirror, a good-sized library table, a short bookcase, and a chair. The first thing I did was to prop the bookcase on top of the library table. It was a perfect fit and ended up being an attractive spot where I could display my favorite books and knick-knacks, all within easy reach.

It was all quite lovely except I found that my single bed had a thin mattress on a wire spring with a big dip in the middle. After a few nights it left my poor back aching. It felt like I was sleeping in a sagging hammock. The problem was somewhat solved by putting one of my pillows in the middle section of the bed that hung the lowest. That helped until I could find a better remedy. *Maybe Mr. Lehman can think of a solution. He appears to be a handy man.*

Each morning around four o'clock I was startled out of my sleep by the call for prayers from the minaret of the mosque, a stone's throw from my open window.

*"Allahu Akbar! Allahu Akbar! Allahu Akbar! Allahu Akbar!"*

(God is great!)

So it began. Soon, along with the call to prayer, I'd hear the bleating of goats and the shout of the vendor as he came along our otherwise quiet street to sell fresh milk. To purchase milk, the maid would take her pail out to the vendor, and he would milk his goat into her pail, any amount she requested. I soon became used to these interruptions and slept straight through the night until my alarm awakened me at six o'clock each morning.

Having had no previous idea of what my tasks would be, I found I was assigned to teach Games for primary 3 through secondary V. That would be similar to Physical Education for fourth graders through seniors back in the States. The schedule was set up for me to see each class twice a week.

With only one Physical Education methods class in my program of study you could rightly conclude I wasn't ready for this assignment. The extent of the supplies at my disposal consisted of only a couple of *British Games* books and a box of bats, balls, and ropes. It didn't take long for me to figure out the game of "rounders" was a bat and ball game similar to our softball. *I can do it! At least I love sports.*

Along with this I was to work in the office typing the English papers and exams, assist Rhoda with English classes for the younger grades, and more or less do anything someone thought I was capable of handling.

The younger grades were just learning English. Some of them understood only bits of my Games instructions, but we managed to work it out with a lot of demonstrative teaching on my part. The children who knew English well would translate as needed. It helped because they were eager, attentive, and seemed to love everything we did.

It appeared to be quite overwhelming, but I smiled and acted as though I knew what I was doing. Perhaps I smiled too much, as I had difficulty with verbal retorts among the girls in the upper classes as the games got going. I had no complaints with their attention to my instructions. They listened politely and showed me the proper respect, but as a game progressed, huge disagreements and arguments began among them about fairness. They involved themselves more than one would have imagined possible in the outcome of the games. Winning was of prime importance.

The girls were to be speaking in English for our classes but would completely forget in the heat of the game. More than that, at times it felt they forgot their teacher was present as well. Since their conflicts were in Arabic, I didn't understand the points of their arguments. This created big problems! Mrs. Bulos, headmistress, would come running out from her office again and again to get them in line for me. *Horrors! I don't like the way this is going. It's all very embarrassing.*

It was decided the students were to call me Miss Myrna, as it was thought Miss Kinsinger would be too difficult for them to pronounce. They said my name with a long "e" and a rolled "r," so I got used to, "Miss Meerrna, Miss Meerrna," over and over. A number of them seemed fascinated with my being at their school and used any opportunity they could find to chat with me. Most likely it was that I was young, American, and didn't sound like their British teachers. They'd been taught British English but seemed interested in learning to speak English like Americans.

It didn't take long for me to understand that the girls followed all things American, mainly the latest American music. With great disappointment they learned that I hadn't met in person their idol Elvis Presley.

Nearly every day someone brought me a bouquet of flowers from their family garden: roses, carnations, and lilies that filled my room with delightful aromas. One morning Emily brought me a big handful of gorgeous, sweet-smelling posies. Later she came whispering in my ear, "Please don't tell the other teachers I gave you flowers. You see, I didn't bring any for them."

During my first week a young teenager insisted on inviting me to her home. She said she'd come for me at three o'clock on Friday afternoon, our day off. As we were making the arrangements she dropped the subtle hint that she wanted her father to take my picture.

When I shared my plans with Mary and Margaret, they suggested in no uncertain terms that I shouldn't let him do it unless she stood with me. They thought he just might have a studio downtown and soon my picture would be up in his shop window. That wouldn't be good.

She came for me on Friday as planned. I quizzed her about what we were going to do. Sure enough she offered, "Yes, we'll go down to my father's shop, so he can take your picture."

"I'm sorry, Randa, but I won't do that," I softly objected. With enthusiasm I added, "I'll be happy to have a picture taken with you and me together at your house. That would be fine with me, but I won't go downtown to your father's studio."

"But I want him to take your picture. I want your picture so badly. You are beautiful! All the girls have asked me to give them pictures. They will be disappointed and upset with me because I promised them. If you don't come I will weep."

Here I met a difficult lesson in learning how to be gracious and at the same time remain firm. For me the funniest part of this whole scenario was that it had to be the first time in my life anyone had called me beautiful. Cute was more like the word I'd heard, but never beautiful. The following day Randa came up to me presenting a big bouquet of flowers from their garden. It seemed there were no hard feelings—all was forgiven.

We were a Christian school within a majority Muslim country. Since the holy day for Muslims is on Friday and for Christians on Sunday, we had off both Fridays and Sundays but held school on Saturdays, a detail that made it difficult to have long weekends away. As it turned out there was an abundance of holidays for various occasions: the king's birthday, the queen's birthday, the king's aunt's birthday, a new federation, a funeral, as well as many other unforeseen happenings. I had no complaints, as that gave me more than sufficient opportunities to go off to Jericho, Jerusalem, Bethlehem, Hebron, or Nablus where other members of my sponsored unit worked. For the little Iowa farm girl, life was exhilarating and at the same time overwhelming, but I loved it.

# 3

## COMPANIONS AT THE SCHOOL

DELIGHTFUL PEOPLE CAME into my life during my first year in Amman at the Ahliyyah School for Girls. Foremost were those I was living with at the school. Mary Harrison was one of the three British teachers who'd been teaching there for many years. She hailed from Edinburgh, Scotland, with a deep, booming voice of authority coupled with a heart of gold. Mary was full of many wise sayings and plentiful advice, of which I received a generous amount on numerous occasions.

In our sitting room Mary had hundreds of books available for me to read to my heart's content, one of my favorite pastimes. Her family back in Great Britain knew she loved books and sent presents of the latest publications for all her special occasions. Among many noted titles I vouch that I read every Agatha Christie book written up through the year 1958, thanks to Mary's extensive library.

The teachers were great friends with the British diplomatic crowd, and I was included in an invitation to a cocktail party soon after I arrived. Mary knew I wasn't a drinker (at that time) so she described in detail what I could expect to happen that night. She explained that people would mill around from one to another chatting. Meanwhile, someone would be coming around with a tray of drinks. Her advice was that if I were offered a drink but didn't feel like taking it, I should respond, "Thank you, but I have no minor vices."

That evening I didn't use her suggested line, but I've been reminded of it numerous times over the years. It brings a smile to my face as once more I conjure up fond memories of Mary and her unique advice.

Sleep didn't come peacefully that night. In my restless dreams I was straining to understand the British accents and listen to their responses when I spoke. It was usual that I heard a reply with a short snorted laugh, "Oh! So you are American!" This party was my first introduction to what seemed to me to be the "British Superior Attitude." All things American were somehow amusing.

Rhoda Thomas had a British father in England and an American mother on Long Island. Even though she seemed more British than American she'd spent time in both places. At the school she was my greatest support, as she understood what I didn't understand but needed to know.

I sensed that her folks, no matter how dysfunctional, had money—not that she looked like it, as she usually wore the same outfit day in and day out and had her hair cut short and straight. There was no time for a triviality like fashion for Rhoda.

She had a car, a little Austin Mini, and used every opportunity to go to Jericho to help out where Kathleen Kenyon, along with her large crew, was working archeological digs. Whenever I had a chance I'd ride down with her to spend time with my Jericho MCC cohorts. One of my best times with Rhoda was the day she took me with her out to the Jericho dig.

We crawled down a steep, narrow ladder, deep under ground, to see the newly found grave of two skeletons: a mother and small child with woven baskets beside them. The baskets had been buried with them more than seven thousand years earlier. They'd held food so the dead would have something to eat on their journey to the next world. It was hard to imagine I was looking at the remains of people who'd lived that far back in the past.

Many years later I visited the British Museum in London and was thrilled to find that same grave completely transferred intact. Kathleen Kenyon had done extensive archeological work in the Middle East and later had been knighted as a dame of the British Empire. I feel privileged to have known her, all through Rhoda, and to have experienced that special gravesite soon after its discovery.

Margaret Kidd was from London. From her I learned about life during World War II when, as children, she and her brother were sent out to live in the country to escape the London bombing. It hadn't been an easy adjustment for the two young ones, but they did it willingly for the sake of their parents' peace of mind. Years later I'd think of her when I read *The Lion, the Witch, and the Wardrobe* to my fourth grade class, as that is what happens to the children in C. S. Lewis's book.

She told me her World War II stories during the long walks we took together. Taking with us sandwiches and water, we hiked out of the city to where we'd find beautiful anemones blooming among the rock crevices in the barren desert. "We're going on our constitutional," was how she referred to our going for a walk. That was a phrase I hadn't heard used previously, but now at times I like to say it, just like Margaret.

We teachers each had our own personal bedroom on the second floor and the use of two sitting rooms, one for our private relaxation and eating meals together and the other for meeting guests. One of my very favorite people lived on the first floor: our cook, Wardeh. Her name, meaning "rose" in Arabic, suited her perfectly in my estimation.

Mary and Margaret told me Wardeh had been anticipating my arrival with much enthusiasm and had explained to them that she would know immediately if I was going to be a good addition. It seemed I passed with flying colors, and Wardeh and I had affection for each other beyond words. She didn't speak English, and I had very little Arabic, but we had no trouble understanding each other.

A fond memory I have is of the night I forgot to take a key after being reminded to do so by Mary. I had gone out of town with friends for a dinner and arrived back late after everyone was fast asleep. Abu Issa, the gatekeeper, let me into the compound and wished me a good night. I realized my mistake, was embarrassed, and wasn't sure how to handle it, as he didn't have a key to our door. I tapped on Wardeh's window; she woke, let me in, and never uttered a word about it to anyone. That proved to me her true, loyal friendship.

And there was Fifi, the very young maid who came from the same village as Wardeh and roomed with her on the first floor. Fifi was a member of a large family who felt lucky that one of their daughters could get a job in the city. It was one less mouth for them to feed and an opportunity for her. She was a sweet, smiling, loving child who said very little but did her work willingly and with a good spirit. An added benefit was that she could learn English and broaden her chances in life.

Last but not least, Abu Issa, the gatekeeper, lived in the gatehouse and made sure we were safe. It was at his post that the screening happened as to who could enter our school compound. His most important task came each morning and evening when the students came and went. He exchanged greetings with all the drivers and knew every student and her place and vehicle. You could say he was the security system that worked with prime efficiency.

Our mail was delivered to him, and more than a few times he looked out for me by paying piastres due. Or he'd go down to the main post office to collect a package I was to receive. This was long before e-mail, and even telephoning was a big task and expense, so everything depended on the post. Living with the British, I didn't mail letters; I *posted* them.

In fact, I needed to learn a whole new vocabulary. We didn't have cookies with our afternoon tea; we had *biscuits*. The big vehicles that zoomed past us on the highway were not trucks but *lorries*. We might ride in a *Land Rover*, not a jeep, and fill it with *petrol*, not gas. A car had a *silencer*, not a muffler, and a *bonnet*, not a hood. One's suitcase went in the *boot*, not the trunk. When we were down in the town we didn't walk on the sidewalk but on the *pavement*. That one really confused me for a time. They never wore sweaters but *jerseys* or *jumpers*. Thankfully we did both wear cardigans. Instead of listening to the radio, we listened to the *wireless*. On and on it went. I thought I had quite enough on my plate learning Arabic, let alone English. *Alas! Such is the task of living with the British.*

# 4

# OUR UNIT FAMILY

WHILE I WAS busy teaching at the Ahliyyah School for Girls, my MCC cohorts were working in other parts of Jordan. Also living in Amman were Hilda and Merlin Swartz, Americans, and with them Reynold, a young Canadian. He was serving two years in what was referred to as *Pax*, the Latin word for peace. Many young men of the Mennonite church, as well as the Quakers, were pacifists. They had the option of fulfilling their conscription time in peace work versus going into the military. Merlin and Reynold were in charge of clothing and food distribution to Palestinian refugees who lived in camps in the area.

The school was near the second circle of Jebal Amman and the Swartzes' house was just off the third circle. This made them within an easy twenty-minute walk for me. This nearness meant I could retreat to them when I needed a break from living with the British and longed for familiar American talk and common camaraderie.

When I arrived in early October, I found Hilda was about to give birth to their first child, which happened just a week later. Visiting Hilda in the Italian Hospital located downtown was my first experience at finding my way walking the streets of Amman. There were no street signs anywhere, and my adventure seemed to be straight up, down, or around. *It's all very confusing! I'm sure to get lost.*

It was important for me to identify landmarks, such as holes in the sidewalk or distinctive posts, so as to remember the turns to take going and coming. I made more mistakes than I'd be willing to admit to anyone, but somehow I always managed to find my way back to the school. Hilda and I became easy friends, and it was fun for me to watch the growth of baby Sondra Joy and help out in any way I could.

On Friday, during Hilda's rather lengthy stay in the hospital, I walked up to be present at their house while the washerwoman came to wash their clothes. A young refugee woman used only her hands on a washboard to produce a spotless wash. No luxury such as a washing machine was available. She spent the entire day wrestling the clothes and hanging them out back to dry.

While I was there, I found plenty to occupy myself. The sink was full of every dish in the house, I surmised, which I washed, dried, and put back in place. I ironed clothes as they began to dry. I gave the place a complete cleaning and made the men a supper to have when they came back from work. Without a doubt, one could see that Merlin and Reynold were not about to do housework.

Since we were around the same age and both single, Reynold and I fell into becoming companions. It seemed he could be the brother I never had. Some late afternoons I'd walk up to spend the evening with them, and then Reynold would escort me home. One small problem: it wasn't good for us to be seen alone together since in the Arab culture at that time it was the custom for even engaged couples to be chaperoned. Our simple solution was to wait to start out until after dark. That would eliminate any of my students seeing me out walking with a young man.

This idea of not being seen alone together was something Reynold found ridiculous, but I understood it living among 350 young girls. The girls were longing to turn my life into something thrilling. Some were already creating fantasies about me. A tall, young Canadian stopping by the school to talk with me would top it all off.

This very scenario happened one warm, sunny day. Since the distribution center for the clothing was near our school, Reynold dropped by to let me know when they'd stop to pick me up to leave for Jerusalem later that afternoon. Knowing that some of my student followers were hovering in the background, eager to see what was happening, I treated him rather rudely as though I had no idea who he was.

Later that took some explaining! Finally I did get the point across. "Please, Reynold! Don't stop in during the school day. The girls are hunting for ways to make my life romantic. When you come by it feeds into their fantasies. I'm having a hard enough time maintaining proper respect."

In Jericho, MCC had workers bringing relief to the Palestinian refugees in the *Ein Sultan* Camp. There was a clothing distribution center, a layette-sewing center for pregnant women, and a third center for young refugee girls to learn homemaking skills and make a little money doing cross-stitch pieces. Here is where Agnes worked, along with a dedicated young couple and Wayne, another *Pax* young man.

We had a boys' orphanage in Hebron started by twins Ida and Ada Stolzfus. It provided care for young Palestinian boys between the ages of five and twelve who were missing at least one parent. The orphanage was a warm, happy home for the young lads with a capable local staff. Canadian Bess was overseeing the orphanage so Ida and Ada could have a year back home in Pennsylvania. They would soon be back; in fact, they were shortening their furlough to get things running smoothly again. Some things were at loose ends without Ida and Ada's expert guidance.

The majority of us were loaned out to other organizations. It seemed MCC could get volunteers to fill needs others couldn't. Our unit averaged twenty workers from the States and Canada. Much as I enjoyed living with the British, I was always more relaxed and at ease with this group. When speaking with the British I needed to think ahead about how to express myself. I found they used a different set of idioms than the ones that came to my head naturally. My colloquialism didn't work with them. That took effort on my part. Let's just say this group spoke the same language I did.

Tina, a young Canadian nurse, soon joined us and was assigned to a hospital in Nablus. Just after the new year, Leron and Wilbur, two more *Pax* young men, arrived to help on a farm in Jericho. Then we were a total of seven young singles.

In our unit were nurses and doctors in both Jerusalem and Nablus. For me two special people were Dr. Corny Unruh and his wife Katie, a nurse, both quite young. His name was Cornelius, but Corny suited him to perfection. He and Katie enjoyed life to the fullest. No one could pull off a joke like Corny. Living in the Middle East had more than its share of stresses and tensions, and we all profited from moments of levity. Katie and Corny kept us grounded, helping us maintain our sanity and see the joy in life.

Our faithful unit leader was Ernest Lehman. His job was to keep everything coordinated and running smoothly. He and his wife Mary lived in a gorgeous, large house in Jerusalem on the road to Ramallah, just past the St. George's Cathedral and the YMCA. The house was set deep back from the road and had four floors and many rooms, with a spacious front yard full of beautiful flowers. For us it was a peaceful retreat. There we could find a bed whenever we needed a break from our usual lives or when we were pulled together for holidays or special occasions.

The distance between Amman and Jerusalem is only about forty-five miles, but the journey was anything but easy. Amman and Jerusalem both are approximately 2,500 feet above sea level, but around the midpoint of the journey is Jericho, which is 846 feet below sea level. This meant one made some drastic elevation changes when going from Amman to Jerusalem.

When I first made this trip, it was on a narrow, winding, mountainous road with steep drop-offs and no guardrails. Our usual experience was to be crowded into an open Land Rover. I'd be so utterly sick by the time we arrived two hours later that I'd need to either throw up or lie down for a while. It took numerous trips, but at last I became acclimated and did the voyage without incident.

Going to the Jerusalem house seemed special except for one small inconvenience. It was the never-ending work. When we all came together, the usual number was at least twenty for each meal. Here there was no cook and no maid as in Amman. To do my part meant I needed to volunteer to help. Mary would prepare the plans and order the supplies, and we'd produce the meals. As there was no dishwasher and the water had to be heated for washing the dishes, that became quite a task as well. We'd assign ourselves either to preparation or cleanup according to our planned activities for the day. When everyone did his or her part the work was handled with ease and efficiency.

I found Jerusalem a bustling, fun place to be. I loved exploring the many holy sites, getting to know my coworkers, debating topics of interest, and the never-ending helping with loads of work. Not that we didn't have disagreements on occasion. When people with our various backgrounds were thrown together for the first time, we were bound to have things to work through. We were not immune to that. I was making strides in learning how to get along with others and in gaining tolerance of their idiosyncrasies. My coworkers seemed to be doing the same for me. *Thank you, God! I'm happy and at peace.* Life progressed onward, as an ever-learning adventure and a never-ending challenge.

# 5

# FROM BABA GHANOUJ
# TO MANSUF

I was never a picky eater. In fact, it might've been better if I had been. Perhaps then my weight would've stayed at a more desirable spot—not that I was fat, just very healthy looking, a good Iowa farm girl let's say. Living in my new country of Jordan exposed me to unfamiliar and different foods. I found it more than easy to adjust to the foods that appeared before me.

Living with British teachers—Mary, Margaret, and Rhoda at the Ahliyyah School for Girls in Amman—and having Wardeh for our cook exposed me to both Arabic and British food. For example, there was shepherd's pie occasionally, a dish the British loved. To me, it simply tasted like mashed potatoes with traces of hamburger.

Then there was the Arabic food, often composed of stuffed vegetables. Known as *warak enab* in Arabic, stuffed grape leaves was a new taste for me. It's rice, ground lamb, and tomato rolled up in a tender grape leaf. I loved it from the first bite, as I did *malfoof*, which is much the same, but with cabbage leaves. *Koosa mashi*, stuffed squash, and *mahshi batinjaan*, stuffed eggplant, are similar dishes I found delectable. All these foods are made tastier with the plentiful use of lemon and olive oil.

Breakfast at the school was routine. Each morning Wardeh set a soft-boiled egg in an eggcup at our place settings. Since I never got good at whipping the top off the egg, I'd smash the top with the back of my spoon, pick off the shells, and then dig in. We each had a saucer of yogurt, which for me was a new taste. It seemed rather sour or bitter, so Mary told me to sprinkle sugar on top until I got used to it. Soon I loved it and could eat it without sugar. This, along with coffee and lots of fresh, warm pita bread straight from the street vendor, was our breakfast each day.

We had meat only a few times a week, and when we did it was in very small quantities tucked within rice and vegetables. This may have been a carry-over from the British World War II days, but also it seemed to be the Arab way of eating. About once a week, Wardeh made a wonderful soup that came to us in individual crocks with tiny lids on top. I presumed the soup was made from the leftovers in the kitchen. Many ingredients were blended together into a delicious broth with traces of vegetables. I looked forward to soup day.

There seemed to be an abundance of healthy foods such as hummus, baba ghanouj, and falafel, which became favorites of mine. A meal that took me a while to learn to like was a dish called *mejeddarah*. It's made of brown lentils, rice, chopped onion, cumin, salt, and pepper and is served either with plain yogurt or a finely chopped cucumber-tomato salad. It's now one of my favorite meals. I learned that each of these vegetarian dishes makes up a complete protein.

My utmost culinary joy happened while on a picnic with new friends. In their baskets they'd brought the ingredients of cracked wheat, tomatoes, green onions, mint, parsley, olive oil, and lemons. Sitting on blankets under the trees, they chopped together a salad they called *tabbouleh*. When it was finished we didn't eat it with forks but used romaine lettuce leaves to scoop up bites of this delicious salad. I was hooked forever.

Bread was highly regarded in the Arab world. Most often, the flat, round loaves that can be stuffed with various ingredients were the ones preferred. In the Middle East, bread is not only the staff of life but at times it serves as fork, spoon, or plate. Nothing tops breaking off a bit of a fresh pita loaf and dipping it into a dish of hummus or stuffing three or four falafel into a half loaf. At the school I observed a student pick up a dropped piece of bread, give it a kiss, and then with reverence put it high up on the top of the wall of the school grounds. Bread held a place of honor, to be respected, and not to be treated lightly.

As for meat, chicken was served only on special occasions at the school. We might see a roasted leg of lamb or skewers of shish kebab when we were guests of student families, which happened quite often. I didn't miss meat and actually preferred to eat the small pies with cheese, spinach, or ground lamb inside like *sambousik* and *sfeeha*. I found them very tasty.

Teatime happened every afternoon around four, after the students left and we could gather in our sitting room. Along with tea, Fifi served us fresh bread, honey, jams, and lots of biscuits (cookies to me). I learned to like orange marmalade, something I hadn't previously tasted. Teatime was my big temptation, and if I put on extra pounds, this is when it happened. I seldom drank tea before living with the British but loved our teatime and soon learned to prefer it to coffee.

Probably my ultimate culinary experience was being invited with my cohorts to a Bedouin home for a special feast called *mansuf*. Yes, it was a goatskin tent. Yes, it had a Persian rug on the earthen floor. And yes, it had piles of soft cushions for us to sit and lean back on. In the center, our host placed a super large tray layered with flat bread, rice, and lamb, covered with steaming-hot yogurt. All this was topped with roasted pine nuts. *Mansuf* is a celebration feast traditionally eaten with the fingers of the right hand, fit for serving royalty.

Meals usually ended with the serving of fruit, which was plentiful. There was always something fresh and juicy in season. Desserts such as *knafeh* or *baklava* made from phyllo dough were delicious but more often served at a tea or a party rather than at the end of the meal. At birthday parties, hosts traditionally set out lavish tables of desserts like I had never seen before.

The customary serving of small demitasse cups of Turkish coffee on numerous occasions took getting used to for me. Turkish or Arabic Coffee is made fresh on the spot in a small, long-handled pot that's wide at the bottom and curves narrow at the top. The coffee is served almost ceremoniously. A maid or young daughter holds the tray of small, very hot cups, and the hostess serves, first to the eldest or most honored guest, then on around to females, and lastly to those in the family.

To make the coffee correctly, fill the pot with cold water, place it on the burner, add one teaspoon of sugar for each cup, and bring it to a boil. Then add one heaping spoonful of the very finely ground coffee for each cup. Give it a good stir. Let it boil up to froth. Lift the pot off the fire for just a second. Stir and bring back to a quick boil. Lift a total of three times. Immediately pour into the demitasse cups and serve.

I learned to always accept a coffee when offered, as it was considered impolite to not be part of the formality. Before long I looked forward to it. After I learned not to drink to the bottom of the cup, as there sat the coffee grounds, I was a pro at the coffee ritual.

Another formality I learned to value happened at the end of being served a meal or coffee. As the guest returned the plate or cup to her hostess, she said the word, "*dymeh*," with the response by the hostess of, "*sahtayn.*" *Dymen* or *dymeh's* interpretation is "always," with the understood meaning, "May you always have the abundance of plenty to serve." The reply, "*sahtayn*," means, "To your health, twice over." These formalities show the love and appreciation between the guests and the host family and symbolize the importance of food in the Arab world.

# 6

# CHRISTMAS AWAY

# FROM HOME

CHRISTMAS WAS DOWNPLAYED in Jordan compared to its commercialization in the States. First of all, the population was at least 90 percent Muslim, and secondly, the Christians in the Holy Land considered Easter a more important holiday than Christmas. When I was living in the Middle East, the Latin Catholic and Protestants celebrated Christmas on the twenty-fifth of December, the majority Greek Orthodox observed January 7, and the Armenians on January 19. So although Christmas didn't play as important a role, the celebrations were meaningful and lasted a long time.

My first year at the school, on the twenty-third of December, we held only two class periods and then gathered the student body into the "hall." Here, the stage was lit up with a gorgeous Christmas tree we teachers had decorated the night before. The students, organized by the music instructor, presented the nativity story in what to me looked like the most realistic way possible, as though the characters stepped straight out of the book of Luke. They read the Bible story in Arabic and sung carols, some in Arabic and some in English.

While Mary and Joseph were watching over the Christ child, and the shepherds and the kings were showing adoration for the baby, the classes presented gifts to Jesus: baskets and baskets of food, clothing, and toys. These goodwill gifts were to be later distributed to the nearby needy refugees.

While absorbing this meaningful presentation I was thinking, *Not one girl has mentioned to me anything she is hoping to get for Christmas. That's a far cry from back home, where there's many a list made out and numerous hints dropped of what is hoped will appear under the tree on Christmas morning. Or there's a pout if something is gotten in the Santa Exchange that someone doesn't like.* The spirit of giving, rather than getting, brought tears to my eyes. *This is beautiful! God bless them, each one, for their giving hearts.*

Following the assembly, the students were sent home early, and Mary, Margaret, Rhoda, and I were left with time to enjoy a lovely lunch. Our daily vendor that set up shop on the school grounds had presented us with a chicken as a Christmas present. It wasn't often we had a meal that centered on meat. It made it a special day for us. The vendor was a thoughtful and considerate man who we appreciated for how he related to and cared for our students. And we were happy and grateful to see that he cared for us as well.

After our delicious lunch, I hurried down the mountain to the taxi stand to catch a ride to Jericho to join my unit partners there. The ritual was that a taxi waited to leave until the car had a full capacity of passengers. That meant we often took our chances at how soon we could be on our way. I was in luck! I found a cab headed for Jericho with only one more rider needed, so I hopped in and off we went.

It was my misfortune that no one spoke English, and I wasn't yet capable of explaining in Arabic where I wanted to go in Jericho. As usual, my silly insecurities set in. I began worrying that I wouldn't know how to explain the way to my destination. But in the end it all worked out, and I managed with little difficulty to find my way to the MCC unit house. There I helped finish decorating the tree and joined in the already ongoing Christmas festivities.

Early the next day we left Jericho for Jerusalem so as not to miss Christmas Eve in Bethlehem. We were disappointed to see the pleasant weather turned to rain as we drove the five miles from Jerusalem to Bethlehem that afternoon. The rain poured down, but across the valley, behind the mountains we could see the sun shining. It was a beautiful, needed rain, but it dampened our spirits, as we wanted to attend outdoor services.

The YMCA sponsored the four o'clock service on Shepherds' Hill, supposedly the site where angels made their appearance to the shepherds. The rain drove our assembly into a large hillside cave where the Archbishop of the Anglican Church gave the homily. We joined in singing the traditional carols, my favorite part. *I love singing Christmas carols!*

This inspiring service was followed by a shepherd's supper of a pita loaf stuffed with tasty lamb, which was roasting in an adjoining cave. What a pushing and shoving happened as village woman after village woman advanced time after time to get more food. We could see they were collecting sandwiches under their long, black peasant dresses. Some hungry children were going to have a good meal of meat for a change. It was no problem! There seemed to be plenty for all.

We were happy to see the rain stopped and we could be outside to join the 7:00 service, also held on Shepherds' Hill. During this service, thirty-two blind girls from the School for the Blind in Bethlehem sang for us, in clear, angelic voices, the song, "Jesus is the Light." I choked up and my eyes filled with tears as I listened to their beautiful chorus, "Walk in the light," and thought about their plight in life.

Hearing this awe-inspiring song brought to my mind that I had many blessings I didn't think to appreciate. I was too wrapped up in my own world, ignoring my abundance. *Thank you, God, for my blessings! Forgive my self-centeredness. Help me to love and care for others as your son did. Thank you for sending Jesus to earth to show us how to live and connect to you. Dear God, use me for your glory.*

After joining the 9:00 service in the Church of the Nativity court-yard, which gave us more chances to sing carols, we were ready for the biggest attraction of the night. This was the midnight Mass in the Church of the Nativity. For it we needed tickets, and Mr. Lehman had given the five of us young people only one ticket.

After a long, tiring wait, the guard started letting folks in for standing room only. I was in front and presented the lone ticket. Our hope was that the guard would be impressed and admit all five of us with our one ticket. However, he opened the door just enough to let me slide through and was about to close the door behind me. I panicked, reached back without hesitation, and pulled poor Tina through, much to the amazement of the guard and Tina both.

A second guard met us, asking to see our tickets. I showed him our one ticket. "What? Only one ticket for two people?"

We looked guilty and I blurted out, "But I can't go in alone!"

He smiled, "All right, go ahead!"

We passed two more security men who each asked to see our tickets and then responded with, "What? You have only one ticket for the two of you?

And each time I'd reply, "But I can't be here alone!"

By this time it was so funny to both of us that Tina and I had a bad case of the giggles. It didn't seem like church as hundreds of people were milling around, talking, and laughing. At least it was a good thing: our giggling didn't appear out of place.

We found an inconspicuous place to stand behind a row of filled seats with a kneeling rail behind the seat. We were getting tired, so we sat on the rail facing the back of the church. This was just after ten forty-five, and things weren't to start until midnight. We kept think-ing how funny it was and giggled some more.

Before long Wayne, Reynold, and Agnes appeared. It seemed the guard got tired of looking at them and let them in without tick-ets. Wayne and Agnes wanted to try their luck farther up front, but Reynold preferred staying back with us.

At last the service began and some priests came marching down the aisle and chanting for what seemed hours. They put new sashes and hats on the main priest and then took them off of him. It was interesting but rather amusing to us in our humorous mood. Of course it was all in Arabic, or perhaps Latin, and hard for us to follow.

More people kept coming in. It became so crowded we couldn't sit on our kneeling rail anymore because we were getting stomped on. Standing was like being in a Christmas elevator.

Around one thirty, some people next to us braved their way out. Tina and I had had all we could take and wanted to leave. We were having trouble seeing what was going on with all the people everywhere and thought this was our chance. Reynold wanted to stay longer. He had the height advantage. We left anyway, weaving our way out through the tight crowd of rather noisy worshipers. Reynold soon followed.

Outside we found it was much chillier than earlier. The rain had cooled off the land. Since our car was locked, we needed to wait until the rest of our group arrived to climb inside where it would be warmer. So we walked the streets of Bethlehem. All the souvenir shops were open and doing their top business of the year. The shopkeepers were doing their best to entice us in to buy. We knew we had many future chances to come to Bethlehem. *No need to shop tonight. The prices will be quoted at their highest.*

Reynold was getting exasperated with Tina and me, as we were still acting rather silly. We couldn't get over our laughter. We bought some soda pop at two o'clock on Christmas morning, the first I'd had since leaving the States. The Coke tasted great, just like back home.

Before long, the rest of our carload came out from the church. We all piled into the station wagon as speedily as possible and were off, back to Jerusalem to our beds. Getting ready to sleep, I was still smiling. I hadn't once thought about home and that it was my first Christmas away from my family. It was becoming my best Christmas ever.

# 7

# TO BAGHDAD AND BACK

THE HOLIDAYS WERE an extra bonus that came with teaching at the Ahliyyah School for Girls. We had many, and they always lasted long enough for great adventures. After some serious thought I decided to travel with the three British teachers to Baghdad for the holiday break that followed Easter Sunday. My other choice was to go to Egypt with MCC partners. That adventure would have included only unmarried young people. Since I had learned that wouldn't show respect for the standards in the Arab world, I opted for the Baghdad trip.

Mary, Margaret, Rhoda, and I were scheduled to be down at the Amman bus station for the 12:30 p.m. departure time. It was only upon arriving that we found that Rhoda and I were missing exit permit stamps, as the Iraqi Embassy had kept our American passports longer than expected. What were we to do?

Rhoda suggested, "Myrna, you are the youngest and fastest among us. We'll depend on you to run back up the mountain and get the stamps. You can do it! You'll make it back in time for our departure." And that is what I did. *Whew!*

Our bus from Amman to Baghdad looked something like an old school bus with all the suitcases strapped on top. What a menagerie of people got on that bus to be our companions. The majority were village women who had pilgrimaged from Iraq for the Jerusalem Feast Days at Easter time. Mind you, they didn't behave like pilgrimaging Christians. Among other things, they were shouting wildly at the driver and conductor about not having the right seats. We were happy with both our pleasant driver and conductor. It was a good thing they each had a sense of humor for the abuse they were getting.

There was a reason to complain, as the bus had more passengers than seats, and three of the Iraqi women had to sit on little stools in the aisle. Later we found they eventually lay in the aisle and slept. They had baskets, buckets, and all sorts of things they shoved into the overhead compartments. *What a racket!*

Rhoda and I sat near the front and wanted our window open as many were smoking. Some became very upset with us and talked about it at great length, not realizing Rhoda understood every word. Later when they thought we were asleep, one woman got up, leaned across us, and banged our window shut. We remained very still with our eyes closed, chuckling to ourselves.

As soon as she was gone Rhoda whispered to me, "Myrna, you're by the window. All you need to do is sneak your hand up and pull the knob out under the window without any of them seeing you."

That I could do. After a short time our window crept back down inch by inch. Soon our companions rediscovered the breeze they didn't seem to want, and again a slamming of the window occurred. This became a game, and I'm not sure you could say who won, but without a doubt, Rhoda and I enjoyed the play.

The road followed an oil pipeline for over five hundred miles. There were no towns, only endless desert. There was nothing to look at but sand. But we witnessed the most gorgeous sunset I've ever seen. We could see the curve of the earth on all sides without any obstructions, just the red sunset turning the sand a crimson color.

The only stops along the way were small places called tea houses. The wide-open desert in the shadow of a tea house was all we had for our use as restrooms. *Not so fun!* We were quite happy, as with us we had brought fruit and sandwiches enough for the trip.

Just before reaching Baghdad, we came to Ctesiphon, the Persian Parthian city of the second century BCE. All that remains of this ancient Mesopotamian city is the Great Arch, a huge, impressive structure. Nothing much was going on at Ctesiphon. The only life we saw was a donkey with two young pajama-clad boys seeking a handout. I was willing to give them a piastre for a chance to take their picture. There was little doubt but that my humble three cents made their day, as we say.

We'd left at two in the afternoon from Amman and drove all night, finally reaching our destination around ten o'clock the next morning. We'd crossed the Euphrates River, and after two more hours reached the Tigris River on which Baghdad is built. It had been a twenty-hour trip, and we'd soon be making it again. But first we were eager to explore Baghdad.

Baghdad, a beautiful city with the Tigris River running through it, had boulevards lined with palm trees, roses, and green grass. With plentiful water from the river and a lot of hard work, the desert had been turned into an oasis. The flatness in all directions was a sharp contrast to Amman, with its seven mountains rising up from the center. The mosques of Baghdad were bright colored and breathtaking. Since the land wasn't filled with stones as in Jordan, the houses weren't as attractive. Most were made of mud, but some were fronted with stone or decorated brick.

Our accommodations were extra comfortable at the YWCA. We each had our own room with hot running water, the first I'd seen since being in the Middle East. *Wow! I can take a hot shower. This is the good life!* The Y was on the bus line, which gave us the option of easily getting most anywhere in the city at a very reasonable price.

On our first morning we left the Y to walk along the boulevard. A limo pulled up by us and the driver motioned that his passenger wanted to talk. A young woman in western dress offered us a ride. She seemed to be curious about who we were. We learned she was a college student on her way to class, obviously from a rich family. After we answered her many questions, she related to us her political views about King Faisal II being controlled by the British, that it was causing the people's unrest. It was a foreshadowing, which we didn't understand at the time. However, in less than three months, on July 14, 1958, the king was overthrown and killed by a coup along with numerous members of his family, and the Iraqi Republic was established.

Even though it was still April, it didn't take long until we discovered that Iraq was very hot. On one of our days we visited Babylon, which was a couple-hours taxi ride south to the Euphrates River. There it was ninety-nine degrees Fahrenheit and sticky humid. What fools we were for going at midday! Furthermore, we had no hats or umbrellas to shield us from the blazing sun. We didn't hang our harps upon the willows, as the Biblical Jewish captives of old had done, but we took off our shoes and rested our feet in the Euphrates River.

We saw the site of Nebuchadnezzar's palaces, the great hall, the hanging gardens, and where the tower of Babel had been. We could see the digs of the temple of Marduk and the processional way leading up to it, as well as the city wall. This site is considered one of the ancient wonders of the world. I've heard that Saddam Hussein attempted to reconstruct it in 1983. One of his obsessions was having his name inscribed on many of the bricks in imitation of Nebuchadnezzar. I learned that one reads, "This was built by Saddam Hussein, son of Nebuchadnezzar, to glorify Iraq." I'm thankful I visited the site when there was nothing but the original remains.

Baghdad had excellent department stores where one could buy anything one might dream of wanting, including the latest French fashions. Any woman we met on the street was dressed from the top of her head to the soles of her shoes in a black robe. But in the store, her robe was over her arm, or her maid's, and she looked like she had just stepped out of a fashion magazine. In comparison we looked out of place, definitely a little dumpy.

One site we didn't want to miss was the Baghdad Antiquities Museum, which had artifacts from before Abram. It seemed unbelievable to see things that were the surroundings of the Old Testament people, and those even before, dating back five thousand years. Later, I felt sad when I heard that the museum was ransacked and that many old valuable treasures, including beautiful gold items, were looted during the 2003 invasion. It's tragic to think they may be gone forever.

My most treasured memory is of the night we strolled to the banks of the river to find a place that served *masguf,* a fish done Baghdad style. We walked along the street with open restaurant after open restaurant, where there were only men, most drinking hot tea and playing backgammon or smoking their bubbling hookahs. There were no females in sight, and we felt like we might be mistaken for loose women. *Not really!*

Mary gave me a quick lecture as to how I was to conduct myself. "Myrna, you don't smile! You don't look around! And definitely take no pictures." When Mary spoke I knew to take her words to heart and follow through.

We found what we wanted, an open restaurant with fires outside on the ground inside circles of stakes. The owner sent us down to the Tigris to select our fish from the many live ones that were tied to a line from his boat in the river. Mary and Margaret wanted Rhoda and me to pick the fish, as we were the ones with tremendous appetites. We chose a big, fat carp, about two feet long from end to end. Our next job was to bargain until we got what we considered a reasonable price. Mary was very good at bargaining and got the cost down to seventy-five piastres, or about two dollars and twenty cents for the four of us.

To prepare our meal, the chef killed the fish, slit it open, and removed the insides. He then laid it flat open in one piece and marinated it with olive oil, garlic, and spices. Next, the chef stuck it upright on the stakes around the fire, which was fueled by the wood from a fruit tree. For half an hour, men waved palm branches across the open fire toward it to allow it a slow roast. This gave it a crisp outside, but it remained white and juicy inside. For another quarter of an hour or more, it was buried in the fire's pile of coals. Meanwhile, we enjoyed sitting a short way down, by the river, looking at the beautiful lights reflecting on the water and at the activities happening across the Tigris on the far shore.

After our long hour's wait, the chef presented us with the gorgeous fish on a board with flat round bread on top. Our decision was to take our meal back to our comfortable spot by the river. We had brought forks from the YWCA but soon abandoned them and ate native style, using our fingers to dig into this scrumptious *masguf*. With intense concentration, the four of us sat around the one huge fish, eating to our hearts' content. Nothing could stop us. We were on a serious mission.

In the end we admitted defeat and left the remains. When I finally gave up I barely could stand up straight. It was the best fish I'd ever eaten, and maybe to this day it's still the best ever. I'll always remember Baghdad for the delicious *masguf*, fresh from the Tigris River, prepared in its own unique way.

While in Baghdad we also visited the beautiful Al-Kadhimiya Mosque. Considered one of the largest mosques in the world, it can hold 105,000 worshipers. It's an amazing gem of Arab-Muslim architecture, decked out in its magnificent blue and green tile. As was customary, we left our shoes at the door and slipped into robes and some padded slippers available for our use. With our heads covered, we wandered inside among the massive columns, impressed with the beautiful carpets on the wall and at our feet. It was truly awe-inspiring.

Outside the mosque, I observed young mothers sitting on benches with their children playing around them. It was probable that they were waiting for their men to return from worship. Something caught my eye, something that would be quite unusual to see back home. A young mother was garbed in her traditional black from head to toe, but with a large, white breast exposed as her baby nursed away in blissful contentment. *Another cultural difference!*

In America we might find a young mother scantily dressed in shorts and a top but with a blanket thrown over her nursing baby. What was most astonishing to me was that I found it embarrassing to view. No one else seemed to give it a second thought.

After five days in Baghdad it was time for our bus ride back. To our delight we had the same two drivers. It was a huge change from the first ride, as we were now only twelve passengers. The drivers seemed as happy to see us as we were to see them. We were pleased that they asked us to come sit in the front seats.

At the last minute, onto the bus popped a lanky, bearded fellow. Our curiosity was piqued when we saw he was carrying an American passport. That led Mary to do her famous questioning. "And where did you come from? You look like you've been in the East. And what is your plan?"

She learned that he was a young Presbyterian who'd been in India for his junior year abroad. Jake made good company for us, giving us glimpses of the many adventures he'd gone through in the last year. When we got back to Amman, we invited him to have breakfast with us at the school before he ventured onward toward Jerusalem.

All the other passengers were men, with the exception of one little, old, shriveled-up lady who, we concluded, was quite a character. She had with her a lamb, a turkey, a cactus, a bed, a mattress, a big potted plant, and baskets and baskets we couldn't see into. *How amusing is this?*

The lamb was in the back of the bus and very well behaved. The turkey gobbled some until one of the men fed it. We picked wheat for the lamb outside Baghdad just before the desert started. All of us were more than ready to become animal caretakers. On this trip the animals proved more cooperative than our fellow passengers had been on the first journey.

I got very little sleep as the trip was so much fun. We spent hours at a couple of places where the men's suitcases were searched. It happened around one in the morning and again just before dawn. Since the luggage was on top of the bus, instead of bringing it down, the official and all the men went up on the roof of the bus to do their inspection. How hilarious a sight it was to see them walking around on top of the bus in the dark with one of them holding an electrical drop-cord light. They didn't want to see in our cases. We assumed they were looking for arms, or perhaps drugs, and didn't think we'd have any.

The stars were both brilliant and magnificent. Having joined the Star Club back in my high school days now paid off. It was easy for me to pick out all the constellations. At the first tea house, where the inspection occurred, I got a glass of hot tea. It was sweet and thick and very tasty. I had fun practicing Arabic by chatting with the tea man. Jake found a cot in the official's room and went to sleep. Rhoda and Margaret slept through it all on the bus, but Mary and I enjoyed every minute of our stop.

As usual, in the middle of the night the temperature dropped. I had my light jacket, a sweater, a pillow, and a blanket, but Rhoda had gone to sleep on the bus with my pillow and blanket. Even in the heat of the summer it gets quite frigid at night in the desert. I couldn't get to sleep after we started up again because I was cold and shivering. I tried standing up, turning around, and squatting backward on the seat, sitting on my feet and legs. I was semi asleep when I overheard the driver tell the conductor something. The next thing I knew someone had put a heavy, warm army blanket around me.

It felt warm and cozy as I had been chilled to the bone. I felt grateful and, even more than that, impressed to think the driver saw I was freezing and was concerned enough to give me one of their blankets.

It wasn't long, however, before I found I had a problem. I felt an itch coming on. I wiggled. I scratched. And then I itched some more. It didn't go away. *What's going on? This isn't helping me get to sleep.* I scratched again. Nothing helped! Much to my dismay I discovered that the beautiful, warm, much-appreciated blanket was full of fleas. *Alas! Such is life in the desert.*

# 8

# PETRA ADVENTURES

A WEEK AFTER the Easter holiday that took me to Baghdad, along came a break for the Ramadan Feast. Ramadan is the ninth month of the Islamic lunar calendar. There are 354 days in the lunar year, and each month begins with the sighting of the new crescent moon. Ramadan is special because it's when Muhammad first received the inspiration for the Koran, the holy book for Muslims. During the month of Ramadan, many a Muslim will refrain from any food or water from dawn till dusk. This teaches patience and draws one closer to God. At the end of Ramadan is a three-day festivity known as *Eid al-Fitr.*

At Mary and Margaret's urging I agreed to go to Petra with some of their British friends during the Ramadan feast days. I didn't know them, and the thought of spending five days with the unknown left my stomach with a touch of anxiety. I found intimidating what seemed to me to be the British superior attitude. But since a goal of mine was to face my challenges and I longed for any new experiences that came my way, I accepted.

Petra is world known as the Rose-Red City; named for the color of the rocks from which the city is structured. It's a half-carved, half-built, prehistoric spot between the Red Sea and the Dead Sea, dating back as far as 1550 BCE.

In ancient days, it was the capital of the Nabateans, who controlled the caravan trade routes of silks, spices, and incense from east to west. They were clever not only in architecture but also in managing the water supply that created an oasis. This made the desert come to life in blooms the likes of which could be found nowhere else.

There are many stories concerning people who lived in this area. According to one tradition, Petra is the spot where Moses struck the rock with his staff and water came forth. Near Petra is where some think that Moses's brother Aaron may be buried.

This fascinating city lay lost to the greater world until, in the early 1800s, a European traveler disguised himself as a Bedouin and found his way through the *Siq* to discover the beautiful treasures within.

John Stevensquill, a bachelor banker with the British Bank in Amman, was organizing and leading the group. Mrs. Kennel, a war widow who did relief work for Palestinians in Zerqa, was going, as were the Majors, a young couple I'd only just met for a brief second at a cocktail party. At the last moment Mr. Major became ill with an appendicitis attack, and they dropped out. Instead, two young men— Douglas Gordon, who worked for the British Embassy, and Argon, who was the third secretary in the Turkish Embassy—joined us. Now everyone was a new acquaintance. The unknown left me feeling a little queasy.

Our car was laden down, as we needed to take all our supplies with us, including food and bedding. The little Mennonite girl in me was amazed to see we had six bottles of wine, loads of beer, and no drinking water, at least not as far as I could see. Most of our supplies were strapped on the roof of Mr. Stevensquill's car. We were fortunate that he was a top-notch organizer and had thought of everything.

From Amman to Petra wasn't an easy ride. The route took us over rough roads, mountains, and desert for around 175 miles. I lay my head back and closed my eyes as we traveled the rough narrow, curvy, dangerous mountain road. To my pleasant, unexpected, good fortune, our journey went along quite safely.

We left late afternoon and spent a relaxing first night at the Italian hospital in Karak. We found it surprising that as far as we could tell the place had only one patient. It didn't stop the Italian nuns from treating us like royalty, with a delicious meal and comfortable beds. The stay felt like a luxurious hotel, a far cry from what we'd meet for our next four nights.

Early the next morning we arrived at the Petra police post and loaded all our supplies on donkeys. Our choice was to walk or ride horses into the ancient city that hadn't been inhabited since 312 BCE. No car can travel into the site, as it can only be entered by a winding narrow gorge. The *Siq*, as it's known, is a spectacular sight of its own. It's a mile-long chasm with high sandstone cliffs going up one hundred feet. We chose to enter the beautiful city by horse.

The horseback ride was a little shaky as the sandstone floor of the *Siq* was uneven and slippery. In my nervousness I was comforted with, "No worry! They're trustworthy. You'll be just fine!" The horses had made the trip many times, and we arrived safely into the inner city.

For me the impressive moment came when, at the end of the dark gorge, my horse took its first step out, and there before my eyes was a massive temple called the Treasury. *Wow!* Until you see it, you cannot imagine how large it is. It's an enormous, spectacular façade cut out of the beautiful rose-red rock, dwarfing any human standing next to it.

Since the camp outside was full, we had no choice but to settle into one of the caves inside. There were hundreds to choose from, so we picked one at a prime location. One end of the open-faced cave we made for sleeping and the other end for the kitchen, where we set up our small primus stove and our food supplies. The middle was reserved for a gathering spot with a bonfire at night. With us lived our guide Muhammad and a young lad, also named Muhammad, who guarded our camp during the day while we were out hiking.

*Camping in Petra*

During our four days in Petra, guide Muhammad took us to many fascinating spots we never could have managed on our own. Besides the Treasury there were the Monastery, the Street of Facades, an ancient courthouse, and numerous royal tombs, all of mammoth size, just as the Treasury. It was disappointing to me to enter the doorway of one of the massive structures and find there was only a large, dark carved-out room inside with no treasures. There was nothing there to give us a clue about the people that had called Petra home those many years ago. Nevertheless, we continued to trek from one end of Petra to the other without complaints.

One day to remember was the day we risked our lives climbing to the highest point, the Place of Sacrifice. It was a matter of creeping along a ledge, clinging to the stony side of the mountain. Guide Muhammad led the way and demonstrated how we were to hold fast to the wall and not look down. At the top we could see over all Petra, a breathtaking view. We found it well worth our dangerous climb.

Up there we discovered the well-preserved stone altar, where animals had been killed, and a trough for the blood to run down. I thought of the Bible story of Abraham about to sacrifice his son. Somehow they got me to lie down on the altar, and our guide, with his huge knife, pretended I was the sacrifice. Of course there were many pictures taken of me being sacrificed at the High Place, minus any blood, I'm happy to report.

To my unexpected but pleasant good fortune, our group proved quite compatible. All of us took oodles of pictures. Later, to my amusement, I discovered Argon had taken an entire film just of me. *Whoa! What's with this?*

Besides hiking, we cooked and ate and enjoyed fires at night with lots of story telling. It felt good that I became comfortable around British conversations and joined in without thinking twice. Douglas, being Scottish, had his own brogue, which I found endearing. And for Argon, English was his second language, or more apt than not, his third. We were content with each other's company and found much to joke and talk about.

Our bonfire in the evenings soon burned out after we settled down for the night. I had borrowed a sleeping bag so ended up being warmer than others who had only blankets. Even then I felt chilly, as the temperature made quite a drop after a hot day. The good thing was it took no time at all to fall asleep since we'd worn ourselves out hiking during the daylight hours.

Personal time was more than a little difficult. I didn't enjoy the so-called restroom breaks, as that involved grabbing the toilet paper roll and wandering off to find my own secluded cave. I never knew what I'd meet in the cave I called mine—spiders, snakes, an owl? There was an abundance of caves, and it all stayed very private. I heated water on our *primis* to sponge bathe when I got to the point that I couldn't stand myself any longer.

Four days later it was time to pack everything back up and start for home. All of us were sad to leave. Argon said he'd never had such a good time, that it was lonely living in a hotel in Amman away from family and friends. Mrs. Kennel thought she'd laughed more on this trip than ever before in her life. We were going to miss each other, our struggles climbing, our discoveries, our companionship, and the spirited talks around the fire at night.

My life changed after getting back. First, Argon phoned to say his pictures were developed. "May I come by to show you?" While we were enjoying reminiscing over the many adventures that the pictures brought to mind, he asked me out for dinner.

The next day Douglas called, thrilled that he had his pictures back so soon. I was shy to tell him Argon had already been to me with his. He came but didn't ask me out, just said, "I hope to see you soon!" That was rather disappointing, as I really liked him.

I never did take Argon up on the dinner date even though he kept calling. He really was a nice guy. I wasn't good at saying, "I like you, but no, I don't want to go out to dinner with you," so I kept thinking of reasons it wouldn't work out and making excuses. It's a little detail of which I'm not proud.

The Petra trip did progress into my seeing Douglas for the next months until I left Amman during the summer. Mary and Margaret couldn't voice any objections since they were the ones who'd set me up for the trip. So it was that the very trip that began with anxious moments ended with new friends and new adventures.

# 9

# LAST DAYS IN AMMAN

SOMETIME DURING THE spring months I made the painful decision to spend my second year in Jordan with other work rather than teaching at the girls' school. Since I hadn't felt successful as the Games teacher, and since now there was a local person that could be hired, it made sense. I'd miss the girls and the teachers, but my experiences would be broadened. At the school, I was among the elite of the country, but by working in other sites I'd be learning to know the poor and needy. Mr. Lehman said he had plenty of work for me to do elsewhere. In the middle of July I'd move to Jerusalem and find out what would come next.

Meanwhile, the school year lasted into early July. The last months were busy ones. I ordered a volleyball and net and attempted teaching the game to the upper grades. Volleyball had been my favorite sport, and I hoped the girls might like it as well. My thought was that volleyball had to be a peaceful game; one where they didn't need to get into huge disagreements about what was happening and who wasn't playing fair as they did with other games.

But no such luck. Soon they were screaming at each other about nothing, and then the ball would get hit over the school wall, landing in a neighbor's yard. We had to send someone to retrieve it, and that depended on the help of Abu Issa, the gatekeeper. *This is more embarrassment. What a hassle!*

Near the end of the school year it was customary to take the secondary classes on field trips. The trips were planned for Fridays, our day off. I was asked to be the second chaperone on one such trip, which I was eager to accept. For me it would be a fun day and another new experience. My first trip with secondary III was to Jerash in northern Jordan.

Ancient Jerash goes back as far as 3200 BCE, but it's Alexander the Great's city of 331 BCE that now is the attraction. Jerash, one of the Roman Decapolis ("ten cities"), had been completely buried by earthquakes until 1808 when a German archeologist discovered its ruins. After extensive diggings, they uncovered the remains of colonnades leading to a forum and a hippodrome, as well as a grand temple.

I found being with secondary III amusing, as every time I got out my camera to record a scenic spot, there was a rushing migration of at least fifteen girls or more to pose at the locale. And they did know how to pose!

*Amman Schoolgirls with Miss Myrna at Jerash*

Since they had previous experiences at Jerash, they became my guides, vying for who got to explain to their American teacher our surroundings. For them it was more chance to practice their English, or should I say, work on their American accents.

One Friday I went with teacher Miss Bedivian and secondary II to Jericho, the city 846 feet below sea level. The day started off well. We trekked up the Mount of Temptation through the Greek Orthodox Monastery, pounding on the door to gain passageway. This monastery was built over the stone where it was thought Jesus sat while being tempted by the devil during the forty days and forty nights he spent on the mountain, as recorded in the Bible.

We saw the *Ein as-Sultan* spring that produced many gallons of water a minute and talked with the refugee women filling their jugs with water. We walked the streets of Jericho to see the Sycamore tree that's mentioned in a popular Bible story about Zacchaeus. We waded in the Dead Sea and ate our sack lunches on its shore. They sang, or rather yelled, songs at the top of their lungs until their voices were hoarse and their throats were sore.

These schoolgirls were not inhibited. When they got angry, they yelled and screamed. When they liked someone, they loved her. Fifteen-year-old Yvonne sought me out: "Miss Myrna, I wish I was you. Every girl in the school likes you, and I'm jealous." It was hard for me to control my amusement. I wanted to laugh. Looking at her face I saw she wasn't joking. I could only reply, "You are a sweet girl. I see that you have many friends that like you very much. That's a good thing."

Everything went well until our bus broke down and we had to wait a couple of hours for a replacement to come get us. It was our good fortune that we were out in the country by a lovely spring with mountains to climb. Here the girls, too, wanted to be in every picture, or have their pictures taken with me. I found the girls so loveable, even though they drove me crazy not listening to my attempts at control during Games.

Our last week of June into July was spent giving final exams. I labored, preparing the English ones and running them off, spending all day into the night one Sunday typing. Our school had the upper classes taking both the Jordanian and the British matriculation exams. It was a big deal, with more girls coming in from other schools to sit for the tests. This meant a considerable amount of proctoring was needed.

I got out of teaching Games, but invigilating exams may have ended up a harder task. It was intense, as I needed to walk up and down the aisles glaring at any attempted cheating by the seventy girls who were my responsibility. It seemed some of the girls' mentality was: "What I can get away with is OK." That was the same as in the games: "If I can get by with it, I'll do it. We'll just see if anyone is clever enough to stop me."

Since our April Petra trip, I'd been spending more and more time with Douglas. Mary liked him, as he was Scottish like she. She'd think of a reason to invite him to eat dinner with us every now and then. The two of them would joke and laugh in their Scottish brogues, and Margaret and I would look at each other, roll our eyes, and shake our heads. *What are they talking about?*

Mary didn't object to my going up to his pension, as one of her friends lived at the same quarters. "Go right ahead. Enjoy yourself! You're in safe hands."

I'd eat dinner at the spacious table with Doug and the rather elderly boarders. We'd hang out in his room, talking, listening to music, and then going for long walks, ending back at the school. The walks had to be after dark as some of our girls lived in the neighborhood, and as I've mentioned before, it was best that I not be seen alone with a young man.

Having been developed in the mountains as Amman was, the city had many fascinating streets and spots to explore. We'd seek out new areas to investigate, often ending up cuddling on a ledge and looking down on the beautiful lights of the city. I never got tired of hunting out new streets and views that at night were magical. It was a bonus to have a fun-loving Scot accompanying me to places I'd not have dared go alone, especially at night.

Around this time the political situation in Jordan was once more unstable. Doug's work at the British Embassy was to decode messages. With all the troubles he often needed to work late. We didn't have cell phones, e-mail, and texting, so it was hard to make plans. One evening he'd asked me to ring up the pension to find out when he got back and then walk up to be with him.

Telephoning the pension was a big job, as I never knew who'd be answering. Would I be able to communicate with the person on the other end of the line? My first attempts made no sense at all. On my third try, Madam Mansour, the proprietor, answered and shouted, "Just a minute!"

After a short wait, I heard a deep elderly voice say, "Mr. Gordon is not here. He's gone to Jerusalem."

That left me puzzled. *What is going on? Why would Doug go to Jerusalem? This makes no sense! Aaah! It's obvious he's not yet home. Now I understand. I think they're trying to tell me it's time to give up and stop bugging them.*

Later I learned he'd been working extra late at the embassy and Madam, who knew me well by that time, couldn't resist playing a joke on me. Evidently it was the highlight of the day at the pension.

With the Fourth of July holiday approaching, Rhoda came up with the idea we should have a picnic. I sensed she was doing it for me, as I was the American and it was Independence Day. When I discovered her guest list included all my friends, I was more than sure it was for my benefit.

Rhoda was a good planner but liked to have someone else carry out her plans. I was willing and happy to do just that. It ended up to be loads of work but was worth every bit of the trouble as it turned out a smashing success.

There were Arab, Turkish, British, Canadian, and American friends of mine invited, including both Douglas and Reynold. I was pleased how the evening progressed. Our guests seemed comfortable getting to know each other and found lots to talk about. We charcoaled steaks on a grill over an open fire, outside the city on a scenic mountainside. Besides steak, the menu included succotash, potatoes in foil roasted in the fire, cucumber-tomato salad, and watermelon.

This was the first time Reynold met Douglas, and his reaction surprised me. He displayed a different frame of mind than I'd ever seen in him before. To me it seemed quite obvious he was jealous. *Hmmmm! What's the meaning of this? This may be a new factor to consider.*

Up to this point I'd thought it was just a matter of companionship between Reynold and me. He'd made it clear he was writing to a special girl at home. That was fine with me. I liked our open, fun friendship.

Was I now leaving Amman and Douglas with more Men Adventures ahead? *Life continues to be always interesting and at the same time ever challenging. Thank you, God. Problems or not, I love my life just the way it is.*

# 10

# IMPRESSIONS GAINED

My two years in the Middle East as a young woman awakened me to the customs of the native residents. Foremost, I noted the importance of the family in the Arab culture. To my knowledge there were no retirement homes. Many families had grandparents living with them. I saw the grandparents were highly respected and looked after by their children and grandchildren. It seemed to be a privilege and joy to grow old, as the elderly were valued for their wisdom. The custom was for the oldest son to take in the parents. The home the parents lived in was open to the rest of the extended family to drop in at any time.

Unmarried young people never lived away from the family by themselves. Even after marriage it wasn't unusual for a married couple to live with the husband's parents. Quite often I saw that a second story was built on the house for a newly married couple to occupy. Then when that couple was more established and the older ones getting on in life, it reversed and the parents lived with their children. Everyone stayed close together and helped raise the new families that came along. Children grew up expecting to have grandparents nearby.

Another indication of the importance of the family was in the names used. Once a man had a son, his friends no longer referred to him by his given name but rather as the father of his first born son. He might be called *Abu Walid* (father of Walid, his new son) instead of *Adel,* his given name. A woman was also referred to with special regard as *Um Walid,* or mother of Walid.

At first I got the impression that girls were not as important as boys. I saw how excited everyone was when the family had a boy but seemed disappointed when it was a girl. "Maybe next time," was often said. At the same time I saw the love and affection families had for girls. The girls in our school were well adjusted, and in no way did they lack self-confidence.

It was the custom for the marrying girl to be considered part of her husband's family. She kept close ties with her blood relatives, but her loyalty and her husband's was first to his family. Therefore, when a couple had a baby and it was a boy, the family knew they were growing a legacy. If it were a girl, she'd grow up and marry into another family. I learned this was why it was so important for people to have boys—not because they didn't love their girls just as dearly, but because they wanted their families to grow.

Since most marriages were family arranged, the girls were not as openly seeking of attention from boys as back home. They seemed content with living with the knowledge that their families would find for them the right mates. At the time I lived in the Middle East, there was no open dating. A girl who had a brother was lucky because she could go places with him, but if a male friend of his went along more than a few times, people might start talking. A boy that might be interested in a girl could visit her home, but if he came often the father would ask his intentions. At least this was what I was told.

Folks were always thinking ahead about finding mates from good families for their children. When a family found their son was interested in a girl, or when they thought it was time for him to marry, they'd seek out information about the family of the girl of interest. They wanted their future daughter-in-law to come from a family that was honorably respected in the community. It was customary that cousins could marry. Then there'd be no secrets to disclose about the future in-laws.

After they put out feelers and concluded a girl would be right for their son, they'd collect the important elders of their family and initiate a visit to the girl's home to ask for her hand. By having an impressive group, they were hoping the plans could be settled on the first attempt. If the girl's family were open to the idea, the women in the family would ask the girl if she'd agree to marry the boy. Often this worked out to everyone's agreement.

I saw the Middle East as a man's world where men and women were not considered equal partners. However, even though men were dominant in authority, the society displayed a high respect for women. The man was the breadwinner, but the woman ruled the house and the nurture of the children. That was her total domain. I observed that, for the most part, couples had certain limited expectations for their spouses. They seemed to accept and be quite content and comfortable with their roles and with each other.

Family ties were close. Aunts and uncles treated their siblings' children or grandchildren as their own. A scene I treasured was of an aunt grabbing a three-year-old grandnephew for a brief second to plant kisses on both cheeks as he ran through the room. The family radiated love and loyalty for each other and became like a dependable clan.

Families loved any social event. Birthdays, weddings, graduations, and anniversaries were occasions for getting together and celebrating. Food was of primary importance with a wide array of *mesa* (appetizers) before the main course. There was singing and dancing with lots of clapping to the beat of the *tablah* (drum) and the strumming of the *oud* (lute.) The celebrations for a wedding went on for a solid week before the event, with all the extended family surrounding the couple.

Along with the importance of family, other dominant traits I discovered and valued were generosity and hospitality. When I'd stop at a friend's home for any reason I'd be invited in and offered a sweet or some fruit, and for certain a coffee. No one would ever think to only talk to me from the door but rather insist I enter and sit down. A family might be very poor, but if someone stopped by they'd manage to find something special to serve. There was no need to call first. Families enjoyed visiting each other and were open and hospitable to receiving guests at any time.

When eating at an Arab's home, I learned to never clean my plate. If my plate was clean the hostess assumed I could eat more, and it would be shameful on her part to let me go hungry, so she'd put more food on my plate. I had to fool her into thinking I couldn't possibly eat one more bite by leaving something uneaten. I learned this after many mistakes. My childhood reprimands about the starving children in Africa—or was it China?—meant I should always clean my plate. Those lessons were hard to overcome.

One very tricky situation I became aware of was that when I visited people I shouldn't admire something of theirs. If I did, they'd insist on giving it to me. It would be a fight to refuse and almost impossible. So it was best to never admire anything in their house or what they were wearing. This was a lesson I learned by default after falling into the trap a number of times. I'd end up with something I couldn't believe I had taken home with me.

I thought I was doing well with this until the time I was given a kitten after excitedly admiring my hostess's cat. I made a casual remark, "I need to get myself a cat to handle the mouse that I have proof is in my bedroom." It was a big lesson to learn to stop myself from ever remarking about how great something was or how nice it looked.

Besides the importance of family and being hospitable, a beautiful thing in the Arab world is the constant reminder of God's presence. In the vocabulary there's *inshAllah* ("God willing"), said when stating one's plans. There's *hamdAllah* ("thank God"), which one says after giving good or positive news. When someone wants someone to do something, he or she might use the phrase *meeshanAllah*, or, "Do it for God's sake, not mine."

One phrase I was critical of was the use of *minAllah*, which is "from God." When something negative or disappointing happens, the person tries reconciling it by saying *minAllah*, or "What can we do about it? It's from God." I didn't agree that all bad happenings were God's will. There's evil in our world, and often we don't follow the right paths.

Something that needs a better understanding is that the word *Allah* is the Arabic word for God. Arab Christian families worship *Allah*, as do Muslims. I find many western people completely misunderstand this concept and think *Allah* is a different being from the one I call God.

By living in this culture I learned valuable lessons in the importance of the family. The ever-present references to God helped draw me closer to the awareness of God in my own life. This, along with the joy of being hospitable and generous, is something that I learned to appreciate and wish to emulate in my life.

# 11

# THE MOVE TO JERUSALEM

THE TIME CAME for me to leave Amman and move my things to the MCC house in Jerusalem. It was to be my headquarters, not necessarily where I'd be working, for the next year. That would develop over time. *With this move I must relax and let my life evolve as needs and opportunities come along. Not knowing what's ahead will be difficult for me to accept. I like a plan. God, I need your guidance.*

I felt sad leaving Amman, as there was much love and warmth there for me. I'd made dear, wonderful friends. The schoolgirls and I had great affection for each other. *I'm not telling them I won't be back.* I was attached to the British I lived with at the school and all the acquaintances I'd met through them. Plus I had my beloved Arab friends. Foremost, I'd miss my Arabic teacher, Lydia, her husband Bennie, and their three daughters, Maha, Lena, and the new baby. *I love them all!*

Not that I was sad to give up teaching Games. It was a fact. At times it seemed more than I could handle. But I'd done well in other areas. I helped Rhoda with English classes for the primary grades, held a drama club that put on some successful plays, did office work that included the English typing, and ordered teaching films that I used with groups. In spite of this, it was clear that it was the right decision for me to make the move.

Douglas, with whom I had been spending more and more time, was going to be transferred to a different embassy. That part of my life would be changing anyway. It's true that because of Doug I hadn't been going up to visit the Swartz family as often.

Reynold seemed quite pleased about Douglas's departure, I noticed. Earlier he'd said to me, "I think, Myrna, it's about time I write your mother and tell her how you've gone astray."

So off I moved, around the middle of July, to Jerusalem. The first thing I did after arriving was attend an Islamic conference in the Old City. Canon Kenneth Cragg, a noted Harvard professor among many accolades, was in charge. He'd written a well-known book, *The Call of the Minaret,* and was known as an authority of Islam. I knew him personally, as a number of times while in Amman he'd stayed with us at the school. Over sixty people from the Middle East were at the conference. Americans, Canadians, and British—who worked in Jordan or nearby countries such as Egypt, Syria, and Lebanon—attended. They wanted to have a better understanding of the Muslim people and their religion.

Once more, the political situation was unstable. This was something we learned to live with, as it's nothing new in the Middle East even to this day. We had problems getting petrol because of troubles in Lebanon and Syria. Also, the clothing for distribution to the refugees was held up at the docks, so the guys were on hold with their work. All this meant the Jerusalem house was full of people. With that followed an abundance of work. I got to attend the conference, but I was also busy cooking, cleaning, making beds, and helping out wherever I could.

Doug called me from Amman: "I still haven't gotten to Jerusalem, Myrna, but tomorrow I'm coming. I want to see you before I leave for London. We'll go out somewhere for dinner. You pick a place, wherever you like."

"Oh, Doug, I'm so sorry! Dinnertime won't work for me. Tomorrow I'm scheduled for both the evening's preparation and cleanup. But I'm free in the afternoon. Can you make it here early? I'll show you some of the places you haven't seen. You can't go back to England without visiting the Jerusalem sites."

He arrived late morning of the next day. The first place I took him was up the Mount of Olives. I wanted to show him the very old olive trees that look like many trees but are often just one. Over the many years, the ground has built up within the branches so that one tree gives the appearance of numerous trees. It was something I had found fascinating and knew he would, too.

From there we ventured through the Church of All Nations and on to the Church of Mary Magdalene. We hiked down the mountain through Gethsemane and crossed into the Old City to wander the streets and visit the sites. By this time I was becoming a good tour guide. I loved showing people the holy sites for their first visits.

We trekked the cobblestone streets, laughing and joking together, just like our times in Amman. "Let's stop for a falafel sandwich, Doug, and then you must try a piece of *knafeh*," I suggested. "I love it! It's my favorite."

Doug's enthusiasm at seeing the holy places and feeling the energy that surrounds the Old City filled my heart with joy. I knew he was glad he'd come. He wrapped up the day by buying some souvenirs from some of my favorite shopkeepers, which left them with smiling faces.

This was our last time to see each other before he headed back to London to await his next assignment. He and I had spent good times together. We parted with a sad good-bye kiss but no plans to write. It had been fun while it lasted, as they say. He would be a pleasant memory for me as I hoped I'd be for him.

While I was attending the conference, we were also busy planning a big event to be held at the Jerusalem House. We were bringing in twenty-nine boys from the Hebron Orphanage for a two-week camp. Out of the forty-three boys at the orphanage, these were the ones who didn't have any family to be with for their summer holiday.

For the five-to-eleven-year-olds, it would be a new experience to come to Jerusalem, as they'd never been out of Hebron, a city about twenty miles away. The camp was going to be made simple to organize since the *Pax* guys didn't have their usual work due to the delay of supplies coming in. They'd be the main caretakers along with the orphanage's local teachers. However, it would take all the help we could give, as there were many details to plan and prepare.

The camp went off without a hitch. In the backyard, we lined up four tents to make one long one with thirty-one cots in two rows, with very little room otherwise. The guys created a couple of makeshift WC's farther down in the back yard. The staff at the orphanage—teachers, cook, and housekeeper—had come with them. Besides the three *Pax* guys who slept with the boys in the tents, there were sixteen of us in the big house. All these people were with us for two weeks. It became a full, active house, especially on bath nights when the little ones came inside to use the big bathtubs. We were more than thankful for the cook and housekeeper who came with the boys.

Our first field trip took us to the airport. Ida, matron of the orphanage, was flying off to Beirut to meet her twin sister, Ada, for a much-needed two-week vacation. This was the young lads' first time to see an airplane. They jumped up and down, thrilled almost speechless—something that rarely happened.

Our goal was to have a daily educational field trip. Other trips were into the Old City, up the high tower of the Lutheran Church to see over all Jerusalem, the post office, the telephone office, the soda pop factory, and the Dome of the Rock mosque. One day the field trip was a simple walk across the street to the modern Ambassador Hotel, where we had permission for them to ride the elevator. The only problem was how to get them to stop. They found it amazing, especially the elevator buttons.

Daily we had game time and story hour, and each evening a family hour. The young lads were invited into our living room where we showed them slides, played music, or told them a story before they went out to their cots in the tent.

They settled down to sleep in a timely manner as we'd worn them out during the day. The problem for us was that after they were asleep was our time to organize and prepare for the next day. That ended with us getting late to bed. At the crack of dawn the little ones were wide awake long before we were ready to face the day.

The two weeks flew by. The boys were cooperative and enthusiastic about everything we did. However, the energy of twenty-eight young ones meeting new experiences each day made for a challenge for us older folks in our twenties. It had been a good two weeks, but we were exhausted and secretly happy to see them return to Hebron for their usual orphanage routine.

Feeling happy and content, I was adjusting to my new life in Jerusalem. It was closing in on a year since I'd first started on this adventure. That was unbelievable. The time had flown by. I'd loved every bit of it, even the hard times.

I knew many changes were happening within me. I'd always been a free thinker with a mind of my own, but being shy and lacking confidence I'd keep my ideas inside. It seemed safer and more peaceful that way. Now I was thinking beyond myself, not so hung up about how folks would react to my opinions. At last I was learning to share my thoughts and think of others' feelings rather than be tied up in my own. *Thank You, God! I like myself much better the way I'm evolving.*

# 12

# THE OLD CITY

WHILE LIVING IN the Holy Land, my very favorite place to explore was the Old City of Jerusalem. Being the holy city for Judaism, Christianity, and Islam, it has special sites for each. I took every op-portunity to enter the Old City and experience the sights, sounds, smells, and crowds that became familiar and dear to me.

The Old City lies in a one-square-kilometer area within a high wall with seven gates. There've been many walls built over the ages, but in the years 1520–1566, the Ottoman sultan Suleiman the Magnificent built the one now standing. The city is made up of what is referred to as four quarters, which is in name only, as they are not equal in size. The Muslim Quarter is the largest quarter and perhaps the most densely populated spot on earth. Besides it there's the Jewish, the Christian, and the Armenian Quarters.

Walking from our Jerusalem house to the Old City took at least twenty minutes. It wasn't an easy trek as there were no sidewalks for much of the way. That never stopped me from venturing there on my own or jumping at the chance to tag along with anyone who had a purpose in going. I was always ready to go to the Old City. Our route took us through the Damascus Gate into the Muslim Quarter's *souk* (market), where the streets were bustling with shoppers.

Here I was hit with the smell of spices and the temptation of candies and other delicious-looking pastries. The streets were crowded with buyers of fresh foods, household goods, clothing, electrical products, and most anything one might need or want. And of course, there were the multitude of souvenir shops with the merchants doing their best to entice me in to buy.

I liked visiting all the souvenir shops, but the ones that caught my choice attention were those that sold gold. The goldsmiths worked away creating their beautiful chains, pendants, bracelets, or rings right in front of my eyes. They used 21-karat gold to make the gorgeous bangles. Not that I had money to buy anything made of gold, but it was fun to look.

The Old City was an intriguing labyrinth of narrow paths with only a few streets that cars could travel. Cargo was transported via donkeys with carts, by porters pushing or pulling carts, or on the heads of lowly men. It's amazing how much can be hauled in this way. In fact, I needed to be very cautious traveling the streets to watch out for what was coming through, as I didn't want to get bonked on the head. For us who wandered the paths, it was fortunate that the porters sang out in commanding voices as they passed by. The Old City is a unique place, indeed. No other city in the world can compare to what this one holds within its walls.

The Muslim Quarter has in it a most beautiful monument, the Dome of the Rock. This mosque, with its lovely geometric and floral motifs, was built in the seventh century CE, after the Muslims overtook the city. All three of the monotheistic religions recognize the spot it's built on as holy for various reasons. It was the site of the second Jewish temple, the one Jesus would've visited many times. The Romans in 70 CE destroyed that one. Some believe this is where Muhammad ascended into Heaven. All three religions revere this site as the place of Abraham's preparation to sacrifice his son.

The Jewish Quarter holds the Wailing Wall, the site for Jewish prayers and pilgrimages. This ancient wall was part of the Jewish Temple's courtyard and was constructed around 19 BCE by Herod the Great.

The Christian Quarter has the Church of the Holy Sepulcher, considered the holiest of places. The church was built nearly 1700 years ago, supposedly on the site of Jesus's crucifixion and burial. This never made sense to me as I thought my Bible read that he was crucified and buried outside the city walls. The reasoning I've found since is that the spot where the church is now was outside the wall of Jesus's era. It's all a calculated guess, just as celebrating December 25 is a big guess as to the day of birth of the baby Jesus.

Nevertheless, the Church of the Holy Sepulcher drew me in for a visit many times. The enticing smell of incense and burning candles, the deep-voiced singing of the monks, and the bustling of the robed priests held magic for me. I'd light a candle, say a prayer at one of the many stations, and be on my way.

On Good Friday, or on any Friday, I adored going with crowds of pilgrims starting at St. Stephen's gate, the gate closest to the Mount of Olives. We'd travel down the Way of the Cross, or the *Via Dolorosa*, as it was known. There would be stops at the fourteen stations along the way, where a religious person would recite for us the event associated with Jesus carrying his cross at that spot. The last five stations ended in the Church of the Holy Sepulcher.

The smallest of the quarters was the Armenian Quarter. What I liked best here were the pottery factories that made beautiful, colored pottery pieces. Not that I had money for pottery, but it never stopped me from getting to know the friendly shopkeepers and having quick chats.

I loved going into the Old City so much that I was soon the tour guide for guests visiting Jerusalem. It inspired and energized me to take people to spots they'd heard about since childhood and at last got to experience for themselves.

One of my biggest temptations was the delicacy called *knafeh* from the Ja'fa Sweets shop. After walking through the multitude of small streets and alleys, perhaps getting lost along the way, I was ready to stop and buy a piece of hot, delicious *knafeh*, a sweet made with shredded phyllo dough, butter, and soft cheese, topped with sugar syrup. *To me it's a taste of heaven.*

The souvenir shops were a fun place to browse. The shopkeepers soon recognized me since I frequented the area and would treat me like an old friend. One day Wilbur and I were "just looking" when the owner talked us into trying on peasant clothes. He dressed us up in traditional garments from Bethlehem. It was a sad story as some poor refugees had to sell their beautiful, heavily embroidered robes because they needed money. We got some good pictures if nothing else. The clothes were without a doubt out of my limited budget.

*In an Old City Souvenir Shop*

Bargaining was part of the game to play. I never became good at it as I always felt they deserved what they asked for an item. Friends told me over and over that the price merchants first quoted wasn't the price they were expecting to get. "Never pay the first price! You must learn to bargain!" After time, I did get better at this, even though I'd go away feeling guilty after haggling down the price.

At last I'd start my way back to the Damascus Gate, past the coffee shops full of old men playing backgammon, sipping demitasse or smoking bubbling hookahs, past the enticing sweet shops, past the shops full of gold, past the peasant ladies sitting along the walls selling their vegetables, and out into the larger world. I'd then make my trek back to our Jerusalem house and all the responsibilities that awaited me there. One thing was certain; the Old City could expect me to return.

# 13

# THE PERILS OF UNIT LIFE

DURING MY FIRST year in the Middle East I taught at the elite girls' school in Amman. The second year I worked with the Palestinian refugees in the West Bank. Normal responsibilities along with our communal living tasks kept me occupied as well. However, it left me with ample opportunities to develop new friendships, and to spend time with colleagues and acquaintances. All this came with a few problems that evolved over time.

Within our unit we picnicked at historic spots, toured with groups that came through, visited local friends, and found plenty of fun activities to enjoy. As time progressed, so did our relationships. Circumstances often tossed Wayne, Reynold, Agnes, and me into the same spot, depending on each other for entertainment.

Before long it was obvious to most of us that Agnes and Wayne had a love for each other stronger than that of coworkers and friends. We could see that in each other they'd found the ones that made them happy in life.

*Touring with my MCC Unit*

Whether it was accidental or intentional I can't say, but Reynold and I grew close. It was easy to happen. We were full of energy and would be off on some common adventure, happy with each other's company. Some nights he and I would go for a walk to enjoy the beautiful weather and the smell of orange blossoms. Our friendship progressed, but we preferred being discreet, never showing open affection as Wayne and Agnes were doing.

Reynold had a motorcycle, and late on a hot Jericho night he might hunt me up, inquiring, "Eh? Myrna?"

"Yes, Reynold."

"Want to ride out to the Dead Sea? Ready? Eh?"

"Just a sec! Is it getting dark?"

"I'd call it dark."

"Good, no one will see me riding double on your motorcycle. We don't want to shock the locals," was my ready reply.

And so I'd be off on another fun ride, seated behind Reynold, clinging tightly to his middle, on our way to wading in the Dead Sea on a moonlit night.

Another unit member, Leron, and I were friends in more of an intellectual way. We got into big discussions about ideals, ethics, and most anything else. We named ourselves Philosophical Humanitarians. The world map in the Jerusalem house displayed countries and capitals. He and I set a challenge to learn every country and its capital and would test each other on our progress. I'm sorry to say I no longer remember the capitals I memorized back in 1959. Of course, along with countries, some capitals, too, have changed.

It soon became obvious that there was a rift between group members and Mr. and Mrs. Lehman, our directors. Among other things, I'm sure they didn't know how to handle the energy of seven unmarried twenty-some-year-olds with far different interests than their own. At the time, they were more than occupied with attempting to adopt a baby.

We saw Mary Lehman as a pleasant but very high-strung person. She was known to start activities, run off to do something else, and leave the first job hanging there for someone else to come along and figure out how to finish. The rest of us learned to watch for this and do what we could to take care of matters. Ernest, her devoted husband, seemed ready to do anything to make her happy. It didn't take us long to conclude that she was the decision maker in the family, with him submissive to her every bidding.

Around this time, the revolution was happening in nearby Iraq. This led to the overthrow and killing of King Faisal II and his family. Tensions were very high in next-door Jordan. Because of the political situation, the American Embassy sequestered our unit into the Jerusalem house for an indefinite time period. It was done for our protection and safety in case of any future uprisings that might occur among the Jordanians.

We were strongly advised not to go out for any reason, which was easy to follow, as we lacked petrol for driving. The gas for our cooking stove was also scarce, so fixing meals became rather tricky. The entire unit was summoned in from wherever they were working so we'd be together. This meant the Jerusalem house was full of people, all with nothing to do but to bide time and try not to get on each other's nerves.

This scenario of sequester didn't frighten us nearly as much as it did our parents at home. While they were busy worrying about us, we were feeling quite safe and secure. To our thinking, the Arab people knew our purpose in the country and didn't hold us responsible for the decisions of either of our governments. It was sad to admit, but major problems were developing right inside our own house.

Things came to a crashing head one Sunday when Mr. Lehman pulled us together for a talk. He gave us an intense reprimand about our behavior, what he wanted to see and what he didn't want to see. He told us he was upset about what he called disunity in our unit.

He concluded with, "Mary and I don't like what we see. Our standards for social life are not being followed. Your social relations are unacceptable. It won't be tolerated! If it doesn't turn around and improve, Mary and I may need to resign."

Mr. Lehman gave us his lecture, and then he and his wife left us with instructions that we were to work through our problems. Our first reaction was: *What's he talking about? Is it true we have a problem? How are we going to get unity for our unit if our directors are not planning to be part of our discussion? What is he really trying to say?*

The rest of the group: four married couples, the three older single women, and we seven young people talked for three long hours. We brought up any gossips we'd heard, feelings we had about others' behaviors, and likes and dislikes about each other. Everyone seemed eager to contribute and was open and honest with input. This led us to gain new understanding and compassion for one another.

Our lengthy session resulted in feelings of unity like we'd never felt before. We all agreed that Ernest and Mary shouldn't resign because of social reasons. If they found this task too challenging we'd urge them to make a move. In fact we thought it was a good idea. They needed a change and a rest and so did we.

For us, the three hours were encouraging and rewarding. The result was that we felt close and endeared to each other. However, when

Mr. and Mrs. Lehman returned the atmosphere changed, and with him we were right back where we'd started. Mr. Lehman didn't ask for any input from our conclusions but became defensive and, with stubbornness like we hadn't seen before, went back to his original message: "Am I making myself clear? In this unit there shall be no social interactions."

As he expounded further it became apparent to all of us that his message was directed straight at Wayne and Agnes. He ended by saying, "No one should be alone together. That is the purpose of honeymoons."

By this time our group was in an emotional turmoil. It was confusing for everyone. My thoughts were running wild. *How upsetting! Now we're hearing from Mr. Lehman what he's been thinking all along but has been too timid to deal with directly. He won't go straight to the source of his conflict? He has to lay it on the total group? If he feels this way, it should have been dealt with privately! He's upsetting everyone. What is this doing to us? How disturbing!*

Later that afternoon I was struggling to read a book on the veranda when, in my perplexity, I got caught up in the midst of a major uproar. *Eek! What's going on here?* Dropping my book, I jumped up in a flash to witness a wild rampage happening right before my eyes.

Wayne was having what might be called a meltdown. He appeared highly agitated and seemed to be attempting to run away. He was shouting, cursing wildly, and beating his watch against the veranda post. The guys were struggling to contain him. All this was a huge contrast to Wayne's usual mild, laid-back personality.

With my body shaking and my heart beating fast, I panicked. *I must get help!* I ran to hunt for Corny, the one we'd learned to rely on for answers to our problems. It was an embarrassing moment as I interrupted Corny and Katie, who were secluded in their room for an afternoon nap. "Forgive me, Doctor Unruh. It's a crisis! We need your help!"

We'd learned to depend on Dr. Unruh to handle tense situations, and he didn't let us down. He came quickly, sedated Wayne with something to calm him, and put him to bed where he stayed for three days.

Tension in our Jerusalem house was high. Being sequestered by the American Embassy forced us all into close proximity for an extended time without any work to do, and we weren't handling it very well.

This Sunday episode affected me more than I could've imagined. It became one of the lowest points in my life. I felt sad, full of emotions, and even more than that, helpless. *Help, God! What can I do to make things better? Nothing is healing this mad life we're in.*

For me, most distressing of all, was the fact that the hardest part of my adventure wasn't with the people I came to serve, but with our own group. It confirms how pressure can build up and then explode when people fail to understand each other. The result for me was that I became a nervous wreck. I became tearful and began having trouble sleeping at night.

It didn't change Reynold's and my friendship, just our public demeanor. Now we hid from everyone any mutual affection. Instead, we slyly met when we could work it out. I felt comfortable being with him, but we didn't want the attention Wayne and Agnes were getting. We were very careful to avoid showing any togetherness.

He was leaving for Canada in a couple of months, and I'd miss him, as he was a prominent part of my life. Deep down I knew once he got home he'd be happy to find his girl waiting for him. It left me sad even though Leron told me Reynold wasn't the right guy for me. I was going to miss telling him anything on my mind. He was very good at kidding me out of my seriousness and getting me to laugh. Spending time with Reynold put a spark in my life.

The summer was flying by. I learned I was needed in Jericho to oversee the women's work in the refugee camp since Agnes was being sent to work in Beirut. It meant new responsibilities. As usual, on the outside I gave the impression I was in control, ready to handle anything that came along, while inside I was having anxious moments.

*Will I know how to manage the women's work in the camp? Can I live up to the job that'll be expected of me?*

For the umpteenth time I turned to my faith. God would see me through these new challenges, just as the many times before. *Help, God. Lead my life! Surround me with your love. Use me for your work. Fill me with your peace.*

# 14

# WORKING IN JERICHO

IT WAS STILL in the heat of the summer when Mr. Lehman sent me to replace Agnes with the work in the Jericho refugee camp. This is a heat like we never see anywhere in the States. Hotter than Death Valley! Jericho, a city way below sea level, feels cozy and warm in the winter months after coming down from the mountainous cities of Amman or Jerusalem. However, I went there to work in late August, the hottest time of the year. It wasn't unusual to see more than 110 degrees Fahrenheit.

We endured this heat without air conditioning. Our Jericho house had a colossal wall fan, which was only famous for its loud noise. Not much happened in the heat of the day in Jericho in the summertime.

Our method of handling the heat was to get up very early, begin our work in the refugee camp at six, and be done and back home by one. The day began with our faithful local workers—Sophie, Hannieh, Hanna Amar, and Salam—coming in for a morning prayer. Then off we went in our station wagon to the Ein Sultan Refugee camp, located a few miles away at the foot of the Mount of Temptation.

I was working with the two young, local women, Sophie and Hannieh, who were both dependable and knowledgeable about our purpose in the camp. Not only were they good at what they did, they were fun and pleasant people. Except for the intense heat, it was an ideal working situation.

The Ein Sultan Refugee Camp was named after the famous spring of water, which is the source of Jericho being an oasis in the desert. The spring is also referred to as Elisha's Fountain, as mentioned in 1 Kings of the Bible.

The United Nations Relief and Welfare Agency, known as UNRWA, oversaw the caring of these refugees who felt chased from their homes in villages of Palestine, when, in 1949, the UN designated Israel a state. For nine years they'd been living on hold, with the unfaltering hope to soon return to their villages. That was their ever-present dream. UNRWA provided for their needs, which included a health and wellness clinic, food distribution center, and a school for boys.

We women were responsible for three projects. The MCC rented a building in the camp from UNRWA where we held a class for refugee girls in their early teens. The girls had never been to school and needed training both in the basics and in practical instruction that would be useful in their everyday lives. Lessons in our class varied from how to write simple Arabic numbers to learning to use a sewing machine.

We also taught them how to take advantage of the food supplies their families received from UNRWA. This might be how to make yogurt from dry milk or how to make a one-dish meal using the distributed rice with the fresh vegetables grown nearby. A bonus for me was that I learned along with them how to make the traditional Palestinian meal called *mukloubie* and how to stuff the small squash to make *mashie.*

About the time I arrived, the twenty girls enrolled in the present class had been involved for three months, coming four days each week. They were just finishing up sewing their own dresses and felt very good about themselves. They stood proudly while I took their pictures in their new dresses. They'd changed from shy girls, who maybe had never held pencils in their hands, to girls who were able to sew for cousins, sisters, mothers, and fathers.

This was more of an accomplishment than when an American girl made a dress because they learned how to take measurements, draw a pattern, and cut it out before cutting the material. This was a life skill for the girls. Here I felt MCC was giving a more valuable gift than clothes or flour. It was a value in life placed in each young woman, a gift that gave them self-confidence and self-sufficiency. The problems of running the class seemed minor when I viewed the end result.

This same center had a needlework project one day a week. Any girl or woman in the camp who wanted to make a little money could do needlework on pieces such as table runners or pillow tops. We sent the women home with yarn and cloth that we'd weighed. When they returned with the finished product, we weighed it again. They got paid for the amount of embroidered yarn on the piece. It sounds rather complicated, but it worked. The women got a sense of usefulness from being productive, even though they didn't make much money. Counting the threads in the material, never by a pattern, was how they did the cross-stitching. We marketed and sold these unique embroidered products in the States, with the profits going back into the work of the center.

*Palestinian Refugees doing Needlework*

It didn't take long for me to know and love the young women in our class. Even though their lives were a great contrast to the girls of the Ahliyyah School in Amman, I saw the same confident, positive, resilient nature in them. It was easy to become attached to girls such as Aziza and Gifra.

I had the honor to be invited for a meal at Gifra's humble mud home deep within the camp. The visit remains buried in my memory since, as the honored guest I was served the head of the rabbit. This was a rabbit raised in a hutch in their front yard and killed, butchered, and prepared especially for my visit. I never would've dreamed that the head was the honored piece of meat, but Hannieh explained it to me quietly in English. This is when I learned to take a deep breath, swallow, and graciously thank them for their invitation and friendship. Then I proceeded to eat the meat I could find on the head of their prized family rabbit with its eyes staring up at me.

One day a week, at a different site, the pregnant women of the camp came to sew clothing for their anticipated babies: kimonos, blankets, and diapers. They sat and made the clothing by hand, but we kept their work with us until the babies were born.

While the women were sewing was a good time for us to discuss health and hygiene subjects. Many of the women were young, uneducated, and innocent. I was amazed to find that most of them didn't understand why and how they'd become pregnant. So we single girls were more than ready to share this information with them.

They explained their pregnancies as *minAllah*, or from God. "We get married. God gives us children. That's what happens!"

We didn't disagree with that. But we explained that their husbands' sleeping with them was why they became pregnant. It was surprising to us that for some of them it was a completely unconnected idea. Hannieh told them, "If you don't want to be pregnant, don't let your husband sleep with you. It's as simple as that."

Of course, we were realistic. We knew the men wouldn't accept this answer from their wives. The layette sewing time ended up with some very lively discussions. I'm not sure who were the real learners, the married, pregnant refugee women or us single girls.

After each new mother gave birth, she needed to bring the UNRWA's "Notification of Birth" that proved she'd taken her baby to the UNRWA clinic for immunizations and had the government birth certificate. Upon showing us the new baby and the proper paper, we gave her the bundle of clothing she'd prepared, with additional supplies, such as soap and towel, all wrapped up in a flannel blanket. This method was worked out with the health center of UNRWA to ensure the babies in the camp got a good start in life.

As winter arrived, Jericho's weather was more than pleasant. It was beautiful. I was content and happy with the work I was doing. Everything seemed fantastic until an unexpected message came that I was needed at the orphanage in Hebron. Leron was in the hospital with acute hepatitis, and Matron Ida was ill as well. Hannieh and Sophie would have to do without me, as I needed to head to the orphanage to help out. *Aaah! Another new challenge. Will I know how to manage? Will I be up to it? Yes, I can do it. I'll survive!*

# 15

# LIFE AT THE ORPHANAGE

IT WAS TRUE! *Pax* boy Leron was in the hospital with hepatitis, and Headmistress Ida was feverishly ill in Jerusalem. The call came for Myrna to the rescue. The boys' orphanage in Hebron needed me. I was on my way.

Sometimes referred to as the City of Patriarchs, Hebron is thought to be one of the holiest of cities by Jews, Christians, and Muslims, all who consider Abraham their father. It's the traditional burial site of the biblical patriarchs and matriarchs. A special attraction is The Oak of Abraham, an ancient tree that supposedly marks where Abraham, those many years ago, pitched his tent. Hebron, a city twenty miles from Jerusalem, is known for its grapes, figs, pottery, and marble from the nearby quarries.

Arriving at the orphanage in Hebron to oversee the work, I found the responsibilities beyond challenging. No one was able to explain the details of my task since Leron and Ida were both too ill to give me instructions. I'd have to fake it. It was lucky I'd learned to know some of the staff when they'd been with us during the summer camp in

Jerusalem. Once again my job was to act like I knew what I was doing. *Thank You, God! I'm getting very good at pretending I can handle anything.*

It didn't take me long to find out what life at the orphanage was like. When I arrived early on a cold Friday morning it was pouring rain. Since Fridays are holidays in a Muslim land there are no school classes. The rain meant the children couldn't play outside as usual, but had to stay inside with stories, games, and indoor play. Before long my ears were ringing from the forty-three high-pitched voices of the five-to-twelve-year-olds outshouting the rain that was beating down on our roof and windows. It wouldn't let up.

At this time the accommodations at the orphanage were in two stone buildings with no sidewalk between them. The boys' sleeping quarters were in one building and the classrooms, kitchen, and dining hall in the other. With all this rain there was now mud where before had been a beaten path between the buildings. This was going to be a challenge.

We attempted to hunt up forty-three pairs of overshoes for the boys to use to get from one building to the other. Unfortunately, we could find only thirty-nine pairs. Fortunately those lacking were for small feet, and the bigger boys could carry the little ones. But—oh my!—how offended the little ones were that they didn't have boots like the big kids. "We want boots, too! We want boots, too!"

Somehow we made it through that very gloomy day. I went to bed soon after we got the boys down, as that was the only warm place I could find. Coming up into the mountains from cozy Jericho was a sharp contrast, and I without a doubt lacked enough warm clothes.

Saturday was back to the routine of lessons and normal activities, so in spite of the heavy rains continuing, the day seemed easier for me. But with time on my hands I found I could think of little else but the fact I was feeling chilled to the bone. My body was accustomed to Jericho's warmth. Now the cold permeated every inch of me.

The stone buildings had no central heating, and the cold, damp weather left me frozen stiff. All the heat I could get came from a round kerosene heater that felt too warm when I was facing it while at the same time my backside was freezing. The one good thing about the heater was that I could set a teakettle on top and it would be ready at any time to provide me with a cup of tea.

Miss Olga and Miss Widad, the two women teachers, left mid-Saturday afternoon for their usual Sunday breaks at home. Teacher Jameel and I remained behind as the only ones in charge of the children. The thought of the rain continuing seemed overwhelming to us, but we vowed we'd somehow survive. It was a blessing that Jameel was dependable, a good sport, and knew the routine well.

Sunday came, my third day, and there I was with the forty-three boys, the cook, the housekeeper, and Mr. Jameel. It would be up to Jameel and me to provide the events of the day. It turned out to be a very long, dreary Sunday. The drenching rain was still coming down, so it meant only inside entertainment. It seemed the young lads accepted it better than we adults did. It was amazing to me how they remained happy and enthused about all the activities we could come up with to keep them occupied.

These children had been nurtured to appreciate each other and to accept their circumstances in life. I found it commendable how few discipline problems developed. We jumped rope, looked at scrapbooks, played marbles, drew pictures, told stories, and played board games, all together in one large, echoing room with the insistent rain beating down on the roof. My head was throbbing from the din of the rain and the boys' continuous high-pitched voices, while they remained happy and content.

The day seemed to extend on forever. Beginning at 5:30 a.m. I'd faced decisions to manage. During the day I found three different caps for Abdulla, who had a bad cold and easily got earaches. He misplaced each, and I assumed he would have none in the morning when he most needed his ears covered.

At long last, by seven thirty, we were getting the boys ready for bed. How they could misplace their pajama bottoms seemed incredible to me. It was only eight o'clock, but all I wanted to do was to go to bed. I was drained of all energy.

After my responsibilities were met and accomplished to the best of my abilities, I finally crawled into bed but found I was still icy cold. This was in spite of having put on every sweater I had brought plus piling on top of me all the blankets that I could find. How I longed for a hot bath. But with no such luxury available, I did my best to get to sleep.

Imagine, snow in Hebron! We woke up Monday morning to rare but beautiful snow. Most welcoming was the fact it now felt much warmer compared to the last three days of continuous insistent rain. The snow was the fluffy kind that hung on all the trees and made the whole world white and dazzling.

Since it was rare for the city to see even one snowflake it became paralyzed by this occurrence. We saw no traffic on the usually heavily traveled main road outside our compound. Mr. Jameel and I grew more than concerned when the two women teachers hadn't yet arrived by 10:30 a.m. *Will they find a taxi to bring them? Can we possibly entertain this lively bunch by ourselves for a week? Even for one more day?*

The snow was magical. No thought of classes was possible. It was unimaginable not to let the young ones out to play. Such yelling and excitement! Sliding and rolling in the snow! Snow angels! Snowmen! Snowball fights! This was the boys' first snow ever.

*Surprising Snow at the Hebron Orphanage*

Our amazement was that for them the greatest attraction was to eat the snow. Failing in any attempt to keep them from doing just that, we at last made them a promise. "If you stop eating the snow now while you are outside playing, we will serve you snow for supper tonight."

It wasn't until mid afternoon that the young women teachers arrived by a taxi that had dared to navigate the slippery streets. We were more than elated to see them. Classes would resume, and decision making could be shared. Perhaps I could find a minute for a chance to sit down, catch my breath, and have a cup of tea.

Yes! For dessert that night we served snow with syrup on top. It was a big hit! The boys thought it was better than the ice cream we had treated them to at the summer camp in Jerusalem.

After my first stint of orphanage life, Director Lehman informed me I was needed back in Jericho during the weekdays. Sophie and Hannieh could use my help. I'd then need to return to the orphanage for Fridays through Sundays when there was the heaviest demand for my support until Leron and Ida were healthy again. One thing was for certain; next time I'd take with me plenty of warm clothes.

# 16

# THREE DAYS IN DAMASCUS

Traveling from Jericho's weekly work in the refugee camp to helping out at the Hebron Orphanage on weekends was exhausting. I was looking forward to a restful diversion. Our plans to drive to the International Fair in Damascus changed numerous times. We wanted Sophie and Hannieh, our Jericho workers, to come with Leron, Wilbur, Wayne, Tina, and me. In the end, the Jordanian government, for some unexplained reason, didn't give Sophie and Hannieh permission to leave the country, and Wayne's plans changed because of illness. Only four of us would make the trip. Besides missing having my friends along, this didn't make me happy, as fewer people meant more expense for each of us.

We were more than bold to be going at this time, as the Syrian and Egyptian governments had formed a union six months before called the United Arab Republic. The new union was leaning toward the Communist Left, forming a pact with the Soviet Union in exchange for planes, tanks, and other military equipment. We knew the Syrian government wasn't too keen on the United States and Americans at the moment, as they had turned their allegiance from the West to the East.

Upon arriving in Damascus, it was quite apparent that we might be the only Americans in the city. Tina was our lone Canadian. However, we weren't feeling foreign, as among the four of us we could handle most Arabic conversations. Our plan was to not make a point of our nationalities. Our station wagon had Jordanian license plates, and we hoped to blend right in, become invisible, and take our chances at being accepted.

Over and over the Syrians we met asked if we were Russian, as Russia was their great interest at the time. We evaded answering and committing ourselves, but if they figured out what we were, it didn't seem to make any difference to them. We found people are people, and when we were friendly to them they responded likewise. They seemed thrilled that we spoke Arabic, no matter how broken it sounded. The good part was that we were communicating. As previous experiences had proven to us, the Arab hospitality shone through once more. We were warmly received and felt all around accepted.

The International Fair was more impressive than we'd imagined it would be. It covered a large area with a building for each country represented. The only Western powers with pavilions were Holland, West Germany, Italy, Belgium, and Greece. Their exhibits succeeded in displaying their countries' economic and cultural traits. It seemed all the rest were Arab or Russian related. We gained insight into the countries exhibited, including that there were some very nice Russians. At that time many Americans looked on Russia as the Enemy. Even my mindset had had that bias.

Leron and Tina's ancestry came from the Russian Mennonites so they had a special interest in hoping to find some Russian food. Tina and I took this on as a project and set out for what was called the International Restaurant. That seemed like a logical place to find Russian food. However, we found they served only Arab food. We concluded that the point of why they called it an International Restaurant was because it was serving international people.

That hadn't worked, so Tina and I went to the Russian pavilion to hunt a Russian in person to ask about food. We spotted the most important looking man we could find, and boldly asked him if he spoke English. He responded, "*Nein.*" So Tina asked him in German if he could help us find some Russian food. He didn't speak enough German to give us an answer, but he was friendly and motioned for us to follow him.

He took us to another man who supposedly spoke English. That proved to be of no help. We found his English was about the same as the first one's German.

Now the two of them wouldn't let us go but trotted off, motioning for us to follow. By this time Tina and I were in stitches, working hard at controlling our amusement. She and I always found lots to laugh about.

After taking us from one end of the pavilion to the other, our new comrades finally found someone who could speak English. He seemed like a very friendly guy as well, so approaching him we asked, "We are interested in eating some Russian food. Do you have any idea where we might find some?"

He was quick to respond, "I'm very sorry! We have none. I did bring some food with me from Russia but another man bought it from me. So it's all gone. I have no more."

Realizing this was our last chance, we attempted to leave our new friends, and ended it with, "Thank you very much."

With that, the three of them begin bowing to us and saying something in Russian we couldn't understand. We left them, barely controlling our laughter, thinking about how human they seemed. In the Western World we acted like Russians were cold and cruel.

Later that day we were driving a busy avenue and got mixed up in a line of eighteen USSR machine gun tanks being moved by the Syrian army. We were thinking, *Here we are! What shall we do? We're probably the first people they want to use these powerful guns on. How did we manage to get mixed up in the middle of their maneuvers? How do we handle this mess?*

We did what we needed to do. We pulled off to the side of the dusty road. As each tank passed by, the gunner sitting on top by the mammoth gun waved at us with a big grin on his face, looking as proud as a peacock. All that was left for us to do was to return the big smile, give a mighty cheer, and wave back with all our energy. This we did for all the impressive-looking, beaming soldiers as they slowly rolled by.

Without a doubt our craziest story happened the first night. To save money we'd taken our sleeping bags with us. After searching out the territory we found a secluded grassy area by a pleasant stream. Here's where we'd spend the night sleeping.

We'd just made ourselves cozy and comfortable by settling down in our warm bedrolls when the police found us. They seemed, I should say, shocked that Americans would spend the night outside on the ground. They took our passports and insisted that if we were going to sleep outdoors that we do it where they could keep an eye on us.

We had no choice! The result being we ended up at the police post stretched out on the hard pavement alongside our station wagon. Very disappointing! It wasn't nearly as comfortable as our first spot.

At last we settled down and got to sleep, but it wasn't long until an official came along shining his high-powered light on us one by one. What a rude awakening! After the third time this happened, Tina got angry, sat up, and spit out, "What's wrong with you? Why do you keep waking us up? Why don't you go to bed?"

It worked! Following Tina's outburst we never saw the officer or his high-powered light again. The rest of the night proved peaceful until the sun woke us up early the next morning.

The disturbing adventure, however, gave us quite enough of outdoor camping attempts. Much to our chagrin, Tina and I spent the second night in a crummy cheap hotel full of Russians, while Leron and Wilbur resorted to sleeping in the station wagon.

We enjoyed the fair with its many exhibits but squeezed in time to take in the usual tourist spots. Foremost was the Umayyad Mosque with the tomb of the noted Muslim leader Saladin. This mosque also claims to hold the shrine with the alleged head of John the Baptist.

We walked down the street called Straight, which brings to mind the New Testament story of God giving Ananias a vision to go there to find Saul, who restored Ananias's eyesight and became the follower of Jesus. And, of course, we hunted up the Roman gate to the Old City where they say Saint Paul was lowered down in a basket so he could escape and be protected from his enemies.

I bought an embroidered tablecloth for my mother at a famous linen factory we toured. All these are spots we were told not to miss in Damascus. We managed to cram in as much as possible during our short time in the city. *It's all very interesting. I wish we had more time here.*

After three jam-packed days and two eventful nights, the four of us headed the 135 miles back to Jerusalem. Our Damascus trip was one to be remembered. It was a little more challenging than we'd expected, but we enjoyed it just the way it was.

# 17

# JERICHO ADVENTURES

WHILE WORKING IN Jericho I learned to know many of the local Christian families. Twice each month a women's group met at our house to do goodwill-sewing projects. For young girls we held two afternoon clubs each week. There was a weekly youth group, which included a Bible discussion, singing, and entertaining activities. It was popular, and often twenty-five young people attended on a Thursday night. They became my friends, and we enjoyed other times together as well.

The Jericho youth planned for us a weekend at the St. George's Monastery in Wadi Qelt. John of Thebes, an Egyptian hermit, founded the abbey in the late fifth century. He came hunting for the spot where it was believed Elijah was fed by ravens as found in 1 Kings of the Bible. In 614 CE, along came the Persians, sweeping through the valley, killing all the monks living in the monastery. It wasn't until 1878 that a Greek monk restored the monastery. It's been active ever since.

Our plans were to leave early on Saturday morning, spend the day and night, and return on Sunday afternoon. We loaded our food and bedding on a donkey and took off for the hour-and-a-half hike up the mountain. To my amazement, the barren land along the way sprouted lovely anemones, blooming in little crevices among the rocks. I never failed but to be surprised upon seeing the beautiful wildflowers flourishing in what seemed to be unexpected spots.

Early on our trek we passed a family of Bedouins taking their time strolling along the trail. Their dogs impressed us with their expert skill at herding the family goats out ahead. After looking us up and down, as though to decide our purpose, the family exchanged peace greetings with us. It seemed they concluded we were friend, not foe.

As we neared the end of our hike, I looked high up to spot the majestic sight of the monastery, clinging across the cliff above us. The abbey, with its various wings, was built into the side of the mountain. It appeared to be just hanging on for dear life to escape falling into the steep gorge below. My friends told me the monastery had plenty of water, as an aqueduct brought water down the mountain from a spring. Seeing the vista above I was eager to reach the site and explore what looked like a fascinating place.

At that time there were over a dozen monks, most from Greece, living a very disciplined life within the abbey. We learned that part of their day was spent in study and prayer and the rest in attending to their living chores. We didn't have much interaction with the monks. We'd see them occasionally, but they didn't seem to want to speak with us. It may be that not all of them spoke Arabic and definitely not English, or perhaps they'd taken vows of silence.

That afternoon we found plenty to keep ourselves busy. Our plan was to fish for our supper in the aqueduct. This involved placing a netted gate to span the narrow channel, which allowed the water to rush through but caught the small white smelts. Part of our group went upstream and shooed the fish down to trap them in the net. The rest of us stayed at the focal spot for the tricky part of catching the slippery fish that were stuck in our netted gate.

Picking them up and throwing them into the bucket was by far our biggest challenge. The process proved more than difficult and left some of us squealing with merriment. Even with numerous attempts, the slippery fish wouldn't stay in our hands.

*Fishing for our Supper in the Aqueduct*

The goal was to collect enough fish for our supper and to feed the monks as well. The day's adventure ended with satisfying success. We caught plenty of fish, more than enough for everyone, and had great fun doing it.

That was only the beginning of our plans for the afternoon. Cleaning the fish, and then later frying them up was a big job, one I got out of by offering to make the salad. Our evening meal ended up being delightful: the fish, a pot of rice, a tomato-cucumber salad, and warm bread baked by the monks. There was plenty to share. To us everything tasted extra delicious. Most likely it was because we had enjoyed our time doing it and used up lots of energy, which gave us great appetites.

During the weekend, while exploring on my own, I wandered into a nearby cave where I got the scare of my life. Tucked back in a dark corner, before my eyes, appeared a chorus of heads staring straight at me. With their hollow eye cavities they seemed to be pleading for my help.

Upon spotting them I panicked. *Aaaaaah!* Backing out of the cave at record speed, I whacked my poor head on a low rock cliff. That venture left me with a huge knot on the top of my noggin and a tremendous headache.

I'm not sure if it was the scare or the pain that left me shaking. The friends surrounded me and vigorously rubbed the spot to reduce its size. All this was a new remedy to me, but to my amazement, it helped.

After finally calming down I blurted out, "How eerie! What's in there? Is it really skulls? From humans? Where did they come from? Why are they there?"

After firing the questions at my friends, one of them responded, "Calm down! It's nothing to worry about. It's the skulls of the monks massacred by the Persians. You know, the ones we told you about from way back."

"But why are they kept in that cave? Why aren't they put in some more sacred place?

The Jericho young people had no idea why they were left in the nearby cave and agreed the skulls should at least be brought inside the monastery. As for me, that ghostly sight ended up in my dreams for some future nights.

Bedding down for the night was distracting, as all fourteen of us were in one big dormitory room on wooden bunks with no mattresses and very large, hard pillows. I had one blanket to roll up in and laid my extra shirt over the pillow. True, it wasn't a good night's sleep, but not many women can say they spent a night in a monastery on a monk's bunk.

Hannieh and I had our best time ringing the bells of the abbey on Sunday morning. After getting permission from the Abbot we climbed the steep ladder up into the narrow, high tower where we found four bells. To do it solo, one would ring two with one hand, one with the other, and the last one with a foot pedal. Since there were two of us, we could put lots of energy into our ringing. As we pumped away with all our strength, our bell ringing echoed up and down the mountainside.

Not that there were many people within miles to hear our joyous sounds, only some hermits who lived in caves nearby. We pulled the ropes and pumped the foot pedal until we were exhausted. The poor monks listening to our discordant ringing must've gotten headaches. I'm quite sure it disturbed their prayers. Nevertheless, the weekend at St. George's had been an awe-inspiring time in the beautiful, peaceful setting of Wadi Qelt.

\*\*\*

In Jericho, it was customary to pop in on friends unannounced. Everyone seemed to be ready for guests at any time. One evening while our group was visiting a local Jericho family I was amazed to see that their daughter was wearing a dress I'd grown tired of and had put in the refugee clothing distribution center. It was a cotton princess-style dress with large patch pockets and a big floppy collar.

The dress fit her quite snugly and now had no collar but a low plunging neckline. She was strutting around rather proudly in high heels.

Of course I was sitting there splitting my sides to keep from laughing. I was amused to see she was wearing the dress I had sewn back on our Iowa farm, in an altered state, however.

Most likely some poor refugee from the camp had sold the dress, as often they'd rather have money than the clothes they got at the distribution center. You couldn't blame them for that. They needed money, and many of the clothes they found inappropriate.

\*\*\*

Jericho's distinction is that it's the world's lowest city and also the oldest continuously inhabited one. It's a wonderful place to live, especially in the winter, when it's by far the warmest spot around. I had great memorable times with the dear friends I made in Jericho.

# 18

## FROM BIRTH TO DEATH

A COUPLE OF experiences left on me an impression of the graciousness of people during difficult times. While working in Jericho's Ein Sultan Refugee Camp I got to know the midwife who assisted the refugee women with delivering their babies. Um Ibrahim asked me if I'd like to go with her to attend a birth. As you might expect, I jumped at the chance.

The time came, and I accompanied her to a small, humble mud refugee home where we found a very young Fatmi about to deliver her first baby. She was pacing back and forth across the small room. It was obvious her contractions were around two minutes apart.

A pallet sat on the floor in the center of the room, and Um-Ibrahim asked Fatmi to lie down on it. Um-Ibrahim sat cross-legged on the floor at Fatmi's feet with only a few cloths, a bottle of olive oil, and a pair of scissors.

Fatmi's mother sat on the floor at her left and held her left hand, and I sat on her right holding her right hand. When her contractions came stronger she gripped our hands, moaned, and perspired. This she endured for at least an hour. Between her contractions Fatmi would turn to me, asking, "Would you like some tea? Can't we get you something to eat?"

At this point in my life I'd never delivered a baby, but that day I decided it was something to not turn into a big deal. I hoped that if and when I had children, I'd be able to handle it in as natural a way as Fatmi. This poor peasant woman was showing grace toward me as she went through a painful time. No one would expect her to be thinking of anything but the task of pushing her baby out.

Meanwhile, the midwife was pouring olive oil into her vagina and reaching in as far as she could to start the head out. I watched for the head to appear. After a little more time, Um-Ibrahim delivered the baby boy, cut the cord with a lot more use of olive oil, and laid the baby on his mother's breast. The family was happy, and we were on our way.

*** 

Another influential event for me was leaving Jericho to go with Hannieh to Jifna for her father's funeral. Jifna was a humble Christian village with olive, fig, and apricot trees and many grape vines on the hills. Her loving father had passed away and within the day, as required, all the arrangements were made with burial following on the next day.

It was my first experience attending a funeral without the body having been embalmed. I kept my feelings to myself, but I was bothered by the odor the body emitted as it lay in state in the same house we stayed in.

The village people, and even some from surrounding villages, showed up for the funeral traditions. The women went through ululation to show honor to the dead. Ululation is a high-pitched vocal sound, rather like a howl with a trill. The more it's done, the greater it shows the deceased was valued.

Here again, at the same time of intense circumstances, the family was caring toward me beyond what I'd expect. They wanted me to be comfortable, offering me food and drink, treating me like it was special to have me with them. *In the future I hope I can find ways to be gracious to others during events in my life when I might be tempted to think only of myself.*

# 19

# JERUSALEM TO JERICHO
# ON FOOT

SOMEONE WAS ALWAYS brainstorming a challenging, adventurous plan of action. As for me, I was ready to join in without a second thought. This one could have been called *crazy*. It was a Sunday in early May, and Dr. Corny, Lorne, Leron, Tina, and I, along with a local friend, left our house around three forty-five in the morning.

Our goal was to hike from our Jerusalem MCC house to our Jericho MCC house. From the Jerusalem house it took us forty-five minutes just to reach the Mount of Olives. We got to Jericho at two thirty in the afternoon after resting for a short spell at the Wadi Qelt Monastery. It meant we'd been walking that day for more than ten hours.

From Jerusalem to Jericho by road is twenty-five miles. We didn't do anything as simple as walk the road, although that may have been impossible as it was a narrow curvy mountainous road with steep drop-offs. No, we walked the mountains, a very rough terrain with steepness going both up and down, more down, of course. Earlier, we'd heard of others who'd done the walk. Later, we found out they'd camped one night on the way.

Just beyond Jerusalem our hike connected us to the Wadi Qelt. The barren wadi descended far down through the wilderness. It deepened into a spectacular canyon before becoming the Jordan River Valley near Jericho. It appeared as a hidden secret passage that meandered along the dry creek bed.

Over the many years it's been used by armies, smugglers, and without a doubt many monks. Who knows but what this was the trek, at least in part, that Jesus traveled, and perhaps from where the story of the Good Samaritan originated. We came upon a spring, a waterfall, and a pool at the start of the aqueduct that supplies the St. George's Monastery with water.

The booby prize had to go to Leron, who started the day out in a new pair of boots. He had blisters on his feet even before we got to the Mount of Olives. Refusing to turn back, he plowed on and suffered without complaint.

We were grateful that at the monastery the monks convinced him to finish the journey by riding one of their donkeys down to Jericho. Leron was an intelligent guy, but not when it came to practical matters. Is it smart to try out a new pair of boots on a day's walk up and down the mountains?

Earlier, when I'd gone to St. George's Monastery from Jericho with the youth group, I'd thought that it was a long hike. This time when we got to the monastery it seemed we were almost home. It took us another hour and a half to our Jericho house, and by the time we got there all of us were dead tired. I was having trouble putting one leg in front of the other as I neared Jericho. Maybe I've never been that tired. What's more, the sun was hot enough that my face and arms were burned, and I felt dizzy and a bit woozy.

We were young. Our bodies snapped back without too much difficulty. What was most important, we were loyal friends and had a pleasant time bolstering each other up along the way. We could look back on it with fond memories even though it had been an extremely tiring day. One thing we knew for sure, none of us would ever do it again.

*St. George's Monastery at Wadi Qelt*

# 20

# THE VISIT THAT TURNED
# MY LIFE UPSIDE DOWN

THE TIME WAS approaching for me to plan my departure from the Middle East, a detail that seemed unbelievable. My volunteer service term had sped by much too swiftly. It was early June of the last year of the two-year adventure I'd undertaken. Without a doubt through this experience I'd matured and learned many things, far more than during my college education.

What had I gained of value? Foremost, I learned to appreciate and respect all God's children, regardless of class, culture, religion, or viewpoint. I learned to be content with my life. I progressed in getting beyond myself, but rather to focus on others. I learned how to adjust to living in a group setting, how to compromise, how to deal with stress, and how to speak my feelings. I broadened my views while at the same time I didn't compromise my principles. Best of all, I'd learned how to show, give, and receive love and warmth. Now

I was greeting friends with kisses on both cheeks. My world had opened up!

I'd grown up in a somewhat closed society where people thought and acted in a similar fashion and didn't easily share their true feelings. These changes I'd made were giant steps. *Praise God! I'm thankful.*

At this time I was working on developing plans with the hope that I could leave a little early and spend the summer in Europe at a Mennonite Voluntary Service Youth Work Camp. At the same time, with the help of my father, I was arranging to buy a Volkswagen from Germany to have for travel in Europe and then take back to the States. I was waiting for acceptance in one of the camps and also for permission from the Mennonite Central Committee to depart the Middle East a little early to spend time in Europe. In the meantime I was continuing my work in the Jericho refugee camp.

One morning Hannieh and Sophie asked me if I'd like to go with them later that afternoon to a local family to offer congratulations. This was a customary visit since their older son had just received his medical degree in England. Their daughter, Samira, who came to our Jericho Thursday Night Youth Group, was one of my friends. Elias, the father, was a merchant and served as the Christian representative on the Jericho City Council. Our MCC group asked his advice about situations that came up when needed. This was a family that was important to us. So one Thursday afternoon, Hannieh, Sophie, and I set out to visit the Farraj household.

They lived in the center of downtown Jericho next to the post office. Upon entering the large double wooden doors that faced the street, we were in a different world. Here was a courtyard with a center fountain, grape arbors, a water canal, and living quarters on the ground level with two more apartments above. As we were greeted by Samira and ushered into the living room, I caught a glimpse of the back of a young man in blue pajamas shaving in the side bathroom. For a brief moment his dark eyes met mine in the mirror as I passed.

We were settled in, served chocolates and coffee, and commenced with the usual formalities of chatting with Samira and her mother about the new doctor, Samir. In came the young man I'd spotted, neatly dressed, and quite good-looking. He shook hands with us, exchanged a few charming words, and was gone. My heart was pulsating fast! The whole scene had lasted only a few minutes. *Whoa! What just happened?* Our visit continued with more chatting about local happenings, but I'd lost my concentration.

That night at the Thursday youth gathering, Samira came with her younger brother, Hanna, who'd just returned from college in Cairo. *It's him! How disturbing!* I tried to give my full attention to the subject of the night, but I'd keep peeking at this gorgeous young man just to find him looking back at me. *What is going on? How can this be?*

It didn't stop there. The next morning Samira and Hanna (also called John or Johnny) appeared at our door to invite me to their home for dinner that night. I accepted and went but remember nothing about what we ate or talked about. The family was gracious, but all I could think about was the impact Hanna was having on me. It was as if I were in a dream. *This isn't like me. Snap out of it, Myrna!*

I'd learned early on in my two years in the Middle East that I could be thought of as a ticket to America. There were many young men who'd do most anything to find a way to go to the States. I'd received proposals, or hints of proposals, from the beginning. Suggestions were made for me to marry a nice local boy. While visiting families with sons I might hear, "Our older son has married an American girl. He's very happy." Or I'd receive a letter more or less stating, "I've heard that you're looking for a husband. I'd be a good one." While on our weekend at the monastery I'd fended off such a proposal to the best of my ability.

It felt offensive to be sought out because of where I came from. I had no plans to fall for any of such nonsense. I'd enjoyed having Scottish and Canadian beaus, but I'd not be having any local ones. Connecting with someone who wanted to use me as a way of emigrating from Jordan to America wasn't a game I'd play.

So here I was, puzzled by what was happening, but adoring this young man who came on so strong it was scary. That first evening at their home he took me up on their roof to view the moon and the stars, I think it was. I felt comfortable with him. Conversation between us came easily. He held strong ideas about what was important to him in life, a trait I found unique and admirable. I responded without hesitation with views of my beliefs and values.

That first night he told me he knew I was going to be the mother of his children. He kissed me and said he loved me. My head and my heart were in turmoil. I wasn't used to that much love poured out on me. It didn't make sense, but it felt good.

Following that night, whenever an opportunity came up, we found a way to meet. He was charismatic, charming, and very persuasive. He took me to his father's restaurant, ordered for me his favorite meal, and told me more about his love and wishes to marry me.

Even though there was no doubt I was falling for him, it all seemed ridiculous, as we didn't have a whole lot in common. Nothing in our cultural backgrounds was similar. It was obvious that he was younger than I was. The fact that I'd soon be leaving the country complicated everything. A love between us would make no sense. How could it possibly flourish? But he didn't listen to logic. He had an answer for every objection I brought up.

We found more chances to meet during the next days. For me, he was like a magnet I couldn't resist. One afternoon we spent time together in Ramallah where we met Tony, his good friend. Tony had a refreshing drink with us at the Harp Park, took our picture with my camera, and then went on his way.

*In Ramallah with Hanna*

It was new for me to meet someone like Hanna who made up his mind and stuck with his decision without faltering. He was very convincing in his belief that we could somehow work out a future together.

My heart took over my pragmatic mind. With him I sensed I was where I belonged. I wanted to marry him more than anything. It felt like he was the one for me.

At last I acknowledged his insistent requests and from my heart responded, "Yes, I will marry you. I do love you! I want to be your wife."

In no time at all I learned that Mr. Lehman, my faithful director, had spent a full day doing his research on John Farraj. Mr. Lehman, the man he was, took his job very seriously. Much later it became clear to me that the information he'd collected came from a source who was upset that Hanna had come home from college and taken over what the man thought was his territory. But at the time it made no sense.

Nevertheless, from his gathered report Mr. Lehman concluded the young man had many flaws and wasn't a good character. According to his conclusions, this relationship between John Farraj and Myrna Kinsinger would have to stop.

Mr. Lehman informed me in no uncertain terms, "Myrna, your involvement with John Farraj is giving our MCC unit a bad name. You're not to see him again. It must end. That's final!"

Thoughts kept circulating through my mind. *How can this be? It's unjust! Hanna Farraj's character is far above any of these undisclosed sources of information. It's all lies. This is upsetting!*

In the meantime I needed to go about my duties in the refugee camp. As for my relationship with Hanna, I felt I had no alternative. I'd have to listen to Mr. Lehman and follow his orders. After all, I cared about our unit's reputation, and Mr. Lehman was my boss. With reluctance I told him, "I give in. It's ended. I won't see John Farraj again."

A few days later while in the Old City to get pictures taken for travel visas I ran into Hanna by accident. At least I thought it was an accident. Hanna, being the strong-minded person he was, didn't listen to my reasoning that I had promised not to see or talk with him.

He drove me crazy! I wanted to be with him, but I had vowed not to see him. In his dominant fashion he took me walking the streets and then stopped to get us an ice cream. All the time he was presenting me with his convincing talk of love and our future together somehow.

My worst fears happened. A Jericho friend spotted us and told all our friends John and Myrna were together at the ice cream shop in Jerusalem. It got reported back to Mr. Lehman and, of course, he thought I had planned it all along. Now I really was the bad girl, not to be trusted. My every movement was to be followed.

I had Mr. Lehman telling me that John Farraj had some very bad qualities and was only using me. I wasn't to see him again. I had my heart longing to see him. I had my mind toying between what Mr. Lehman was telling me about his character and my own doubts about how this love could be for real.

I wanted it to be true; that Hanna loved me as much as he professed. But could I trust something that happened that fast? Was I being fooled, falling into a trap and being used? Or was I going to let a love get away that felt so right? I was in turmoil, very confused.

Notification came that I'd been accepted into a youth camp in Germany. With Mr. Lehman's high recommendation, MCC gave me permission to leave early for Europe. In the meantime my every movement was being watched. I felt like a prisoner.

As my departure date came closer, Mr. Lehman insisted that before I left the country I must make myself clear and completely cut my relationship with John Farraj. Being pinned down as I was and wanting to keep a good name with MCC, I succumbed to the power over me. With distressful pain I went with him and his wife to the Farraj residence to back out of any promises I'd led Hanna to believe.

The only way I could get through the encounter was to turn my heart to stone and become an actor playing a role. So before Hanna, his mother, and Mr. and Mrs. Lehman, I stated, "Hanna, this is my good-bye to you. I won't see you again. I'm here to say that I'm backing out of my promise to marry you. Forgive me, please."

Shortly following that miserable visit I received a passionate letter from Hanna, a letter that left me both crying and laughing. *This guy is a once in a lifetime guy! Am I going to lose him?*

Mulling over the possibilities of how our love could be realized, I concluded a future for us together was out of the question. He was a young man with his full life ahead and the dreams his family hoped for him. I was soon going to be back in the States. How could a love between us ever work out? Was I to stand in the way of his future? It would be best to put it completely to an end. *Be strong, Myrna! Do the right thing.*

I wrote him a parting reply that I sent off just before I departed by taxi to Beirut to catch a boat for Europe. *This will be the end! It's painful to cut it off and say good-bye forever, but it's the only way. It's the right thing to do.*

I felt brokenhearted! Having new horizons might be my only relief. My heart needed to heal. At the same time, deep down, I knew I would marry Hanna Farraj one day.

*Hanna E. Farraj*
*5th of July 1959*
*Jericho*
*"God bless our Love"*

*My dearest Myrna,*

*I don't know whether this letter will be welcome or not but I feel it's my duty to write. We have been close friends for a short time and I remember we both agreed that we would be to each other forever, and that we would meet about four times weekly, just as friends. Sometimes it is very hard to forget that I love you and treat you just as a friend Myrna——!!*

*But I know now that you have been patient and understanding and up to now our friendship has been that sweetest thing I have ever known.*

*When I met you last time in our home I looked in your face and tried to see whether you were sincere and whether you had true love in your heart for me. I thought the best way to find out would be to see if you would think I was worth waiting for.*

*When I came out and saw you standing out with "Lehmans" I thought you looked so sad on your self. I don't know just what was saying to you, but you know very well that you are really and truly the most kindest and sincere beloved. I know very well that you love me. . . . . .you love me . . . . . .you love me, and you'll never forget the lovely time that we spent together, but I think you were forced to say what you said about not seeing me.... . in Jordan.*

*I know very well that my love to you will never change, because it is the true feeling towards you now, tomorrow and forever. So my darling Myrna tonight before you go to sleep won't you just kneel and say "FORGIVE US OUR TRESPASSES AS WE FORGIVE THOSE WHO TRESPASS AGAINST US."*

*I don't know if you read what I wrote to you in your "Autograph" but now I would like to say something. . . . . .I meant it . . . . ..do you remember it . . . . . .. I think you forgot it. . . . . ..*

*I SHALL LOVE YOU TO THE END, AND BEYOND.*

*Yours forever,*
*Hanna E. Farraj*
*XXX*

*I am waiting your answer. . . ...I don't care if it is from Jordan, or from Germany. . . ...but please make it soon!!! Won't you Darling.*

*I saw in the post office a message from your parents. I don't know what did they answer but anyway please if you meet them, tell them that Hanna was loving you truly and with all his heart and he shall forever.*

*Wednesday the 8ᵗʰ*

*My dear Hanna,*

*I got your letter on Sunday and I was happy that you wrote to me. I, too, remember the nice times we had together and they will always remain in my mind as sweet memories.*

*The first night I was with you, you talked about Love. One thing you said was that you thought whether or not our love ends in marriage it will be easier to go through life knowing we loved each other.*

*I am a little mixed up right now. I liked you very much and trusted you, and I learned to love you also in the short time I knew you. However, I feel in life sometimes a person has to give up even some of their own wants and desires if they feel it may be better that way. This is the way I feel now about our love. It may be better for both of us, if we part our ways and keep in our hearts a special corner for our love.*

*I don't know if it's too much to ask you to forgive me for making any promises to you before I realized what they meant. You did many nice things for me. I will always remember you with love. I hope that because we have known each other and loved we will be better people and worth more in life. That way God can bless our love.*

*So I think now I shall say Good by to you.—I will always remember you.*

*With love, Myrna*

*P.S. I will give you my Germany address because you asked for it on the phone but you realize this does not mean any promises hold true.*

*Myrna Kinsinger*
*M. V. S. "Siedlung auf der Aue"*
*Pfeddersheim bei Worms, GERMANY*

# 21

---

# DEPARTURE

IT WAS DISCOURAGING to hear that taxis wouldn't cross countries' borders. That meant it took three cabs to get me to my scheduled sailing ship. My first ride was from Jerusalem to the Syrian border. The second one that I needed to catch took me through the Syrian countryside and its capital, Damascus. And at long last my final ride was from the Syrian-Lebanese border into Beirut. All three depended on full passenger loads before starting out on their respective journeys.

It was more than bothersome to leave one taxi, find the next, and to remain patient until that vehicle was full and ready to get on its way. Along with that inconvenience, it wasn't a comfortable ride to be squeezed in the back seat between two big men smoking cigarettes. But that's what I had to endure upon leaving my two-year adventure in the Middle East.

These taxi changes I made while lugging along two oversized suitcases plus a smaller, normal-sized bag. I had packed in haste the rest of my things in a large steamer trunk that Leron was sharing with me. After two years it was unbelievable how many souvenirs I'd collected for gifts at home. Mr. Lehman would see that the trunk got sent to America.

After reaching Beirut I had two nights to spend before my Greek ship was scheduled to sail from Beirut to where I'd disembark in Vienna. It was my good fortune that a cousin, Owen Gingerich, Professor of Astronomy at Harvard, had returned to the American University of Beirut to do follow-up photography with the Lee Observatory's telescope.

He took me under his wing and gave me a good look around the university. With the tour I got a marvelous chance to see the telescope that he spent working on for many long hours. I learned about the restoration work Dr. Gingerich had done over the last four years at the university in the astronomy department. He and a local colleague had brought new life into the program by starting "Open Nights Observations" along with developing an impressive astronomical library.

The next day we drove down to Tyre and Sidon and saw the massive old Castle Beaufort near the Syrian border. This was a crusader fortress from the twelfth century CE with a long history of captures and recaptures. It was a lovely drive with a pleasant picnic lunch along the way. The day felt therapeutic, which I needed.

Early the next morning it was down to the Beirut pier to board the huge Greek ship for my seven-day sail. I was traveling Tourist Class, a fancy way to say third class, which meant I'd be sharing a cabin with five other females. However, my cabin was still occupied. I had a seven- (or perhaps eight-) hour wait until we docked at Cyprus, where the present occupants of the cabin would disembark. That left me with the dilemma of how to spend the day on deck with my cumbersome luggage.

Making friends while traveling alone aboard a ship ended up being much easier that I had expected. Too easy! There was the Greek student, the Lebanese playboy, an Egyptian travel agent, a Greek Cypriot, and a New Zealand sailor—all male, of course! The debonair playboy, who professed he owned a taxi company in

Beirut, insisted on renting me a deck chair for the day. That was a good thing as it was something I couldn't afford, and it gave me a place to settle my suitcases and myself until I could get into my cabin.

Not so pleasant was the fact that he was on a chair next to mine. I wasn't in the mood to chitchat with anyone about anything. My biggest desire was to be alone. My head was spinning. I needed time to think about all that had happened to me before my hasty departure from Jordan. While lying back on my deck chair with my eyes closed, pretending to be asleep, I was thinking.

*That's it! It will be over. It was painful to write that letter to Hanna, but I needed to do it to let him know he is free of the commitment.*

*His family will be relieved. He's still a college student and has his whole life ahead of him. He's smart, and they have high hopes and plans for him.*

*He insisted he loved me, but how long will that last? With his personality and good looks there are far more accomplished and good looking girls than Myrna Kinsinger who he can fall in love with and marry. I must be reasonable. John Farraj must be put out of my mind.*

*But my heart aches. I don't want it to be over. God, I pray for you to direct my life. Your will be done.*

The ship was beyond full. Since the Italian lines were on strike, more passengers kept coming aboard our Greek ship. The deck was crowded. Masses of people were camping out on deck with all their things: luggage, sleeping blankets, and food. It wasn't easy to walk the deck. I felt I was walking through people's private homes. Men, women, and little children stared me down. They wanted their privacy.

I saw that I was lucky to be in a cabin, even if it was for six. Mine was a top bunk, and I needed to put my suitcases up with me since the room was too small for them to be put anywhere else. They had secure locks and stayed right where I put them. There wasn't much room left for me. The cabin wasn't pleasant, so I went there only to sleep. None of my mates spoke any language I spoke, and they all seemed to be seasick. Very depressing! I religiously took my Dramamine.

The crowded ship made me feel lonely. Not that I wanted companions—just a place to be alone. Lonely wasn't my typical feeling. It seemed strange that masses of people made me lonely. As far as I could conclude, there were no other Americans on our ship, at least not on my deck. I heard no English, except of course from those guys who tried to befriend me. They didn't help my loneliness.

By chance I was blessed to cross paths with a British couple and two single girls who had embarked from Cyprus where they'd been teaching. Since I'd lived with British and knew their ways, being with them felt comfortable and secure. They were ready to embrace me and include me on the day trips at our stops. It would've saved me money to accept an admirer's invitation, but I wasn't in the mood. The stops we made were in Alexandria, Piraeus, and Brindisi before docking in Venice. A driver would be meeting me there with my new Volkswagen.

In Alexandria we went off the ship to tour a famous museum, the Catacombs, with its many coffins and tombs, and King Farouk's Palace. It was surprising to learn that Farouk had assumed power of Egypt at age sixteen. The elaborate grounds and buildings where he had lived seemed magnificent. *Now at least I can say I've been to Egypt.*

Docking two days in Piraeus offered us close access to the must-see city of Athens. Sheila, my new British friend, and I hopped the subway twice for a thirty-minute ride into Athens. We trudged up the hill to walk the famous Acropolis. There, among other excavated ruins, we found the beautiful Parthenon that dates back to 438 BCE. Even though it was a pleasant July day we saw only one other tourist making the same hike up to view the ancient remains.

Great excitement sprung up among the many passengers as our ship ventured through the Corinth Canal in the Aegean Sea. The canal is four miles long and only seventy feet wide. The width of our ship had to have been sixty-nine feet or more, as we saw no room on the sides as we slowly crept through.

Our next stop was at toasty-warm Brindisi in southern Italy. This port was the most fun, with the streets full of colorful Italians and a chance to get a gelato. Here, we girls received a number of wolf whistles. *There's nothing like a wolf whistle to lift the spirits and put a smile on my face!* All these stops provided great distractions for my troubled mind.

When we reached Venice, our place of arrival, my anxieties kicked in. Thousands of people! Peering down from the ship rail at the masses I couldn't imagine how I'd ever find Paul, the Pax guy, who drove my VW down from Frankfort to pick me up.

Once more disembarkation took hours. Finally, I got through the lengthy formalities. The British friend had gotten off the ship earlier. When he got back he consoled me, "Myrna, I'm quite sure I spotted your driver. Who but an American would be wearing lederhosen (leather breeches) in Venice?"

It was late afternoon before I finally got off the boat. I laughed as I spotted him just as the Brit had predicted. It was a very-tall Paul in lederhosen, standing under a tree holding a sign that read, "Myrna Kinsinger." Things do work out.

After a quick stop at the magnificent Byzantine cathedral, Saint Mark's Basilica—where to our amusement we found as many Americans as pigeons—we ended the evening with a gondola ride, a must-do when in Venice. I spent a blissful night in a tiny hotel room where I took a long, hot shower, shampooed my hair, and at last was alone.

The following day it was off through the gorgeous Austrian countryside with its beautiful lakes and mountains. My eyes soaked in the luscious, green growth, a sharp contrast from the sands of the Middle East.

After spending one short night in Mozart's hometown, Salzburg, the next day we were in Frankfurt, Germany, where Paul lived and worked. It was time for me to do my own driving. Only a couple hours drive and I'd be in the small village of Pfeddersheim near Worms to begin my six weeks at the Youth Work Camp.

Driving on the autobahn needed my full concentration but still gave me time to think. *I wonder what camp will be like? Who will be the other campers? I have no idea what we'll be doing. I'm looking forward to it. It'll be good for me. Maybe my mind will escape from Jericho. That's a good thing! I need new horizons.* Another adventure was about to begin. I was more than ready!

# 22

# THE SUMMER CAMP

CAMP LIFE IN Pfeddersheim was an answer to my prayers. The youth were warmhearted and full of life, and the work was intense. After the first day I was drop-dead tired, having shoveled dirt into a wheelbarrow all day long. The blisters on my hands were painfully seeping liquid, but I was content and happy. The moments occupied my total mind. There was no time to regret what I'd left behind. No time to dwell on a love that had felt so right. I was too occupied to mull over my decisions of what might have been. My time in the Middle East was behind me. The Youth Work Camp was a new chapter in my life.

Pfeddersheim, a proud little German town, was taking on the building of a settlement of fourteen houses for East German refugee families who needed financial help. Before a family could move in, its members had to put in a certain number of work hours. The hours we worked could be applied toward the future occupant's time, and the money we earned would be used for something for the entire settlement. Each week we worked five eight-hour days. That gave us the weekend for touring or whatever else we dreamed up to occupy ourselves.

We totaled twenty campers, coming from Holland, Germany, France, Switzerland, Greece, England, and America. In quick fashion, Dutch Tinika and I connected and partnered both in work and fun. Tinika had a bubbly, positive personality that I found most enjoyable. We hit it off from the beginning and became close buddies, finding pleasure in every job we were assigned.

Peter, also from Holland, spent his time with us whenever possible and kept us happy. He worked hard at teaching me Dutch phrases. To this day I'm known to recite, *"De maan is achter de wolken"* ("The moon is behind the clouds").

*With Tinnika and Peter in Pfeddersheim Camp*

I was elated to find Dick from Minnesota, and his wife Rita, as part of our camp. I had met Dick the summer before when he came to the Islamic Conference in Jerusalem from teaching in Lebanon. He left there to go home to marry Rita. They both had taught the past year in Sidon. Since their first wedding anniversary fell during camp I offered them my VW to get away for the weekend. It felt good to give them that joy.

The guys and we girls manually did all the same work, nothing by machine. We loaded the cement mixer with sand, gravel, cement, and water and then turned it by hand until it was ready to pour out into the wheelbarrow and be taken to its needed spot. We hammered and nailed siding and floorboards. We dug ditches, and we filled ditches back up. We painted everything possible, including the office wagon. Pfeddersheim couldn't have found more diligent but happy, contented workers.

Of the houses being built, we lived in two. They weren't completely finished but far enough along for our comfort. There was a cot for everyone, but nothing more. We lived out of our suitcases. No one had any concerns about how one looked or what one wore. It was to our advantage that we had no mirrors on the site. What we did have were twenty sparkling, cheerful faces.

I'd say that our biggest inconvenience was that the houses didn't yet have their indoor plumbing. We had to use an outhouse, a typical wooden two-hole shed with a quarter moon cut out above the door. There were two of them, one for us girls and the second for the guys.

The girls' house had the useable kitchen and dining room. Each day, two of us were assigned for meal preparations. We'd prepare two breakfasts, one early and the other at nine, followed by a lunch and a dinner. There was a bounty of tempting, heavy dark German bread that proved delicious with honey and jams and also made excellent sandwiches. Because of our strenuous physical activity we were good eaters. It was our luck that we had an abundance of delicious, fresh food brought in each day to enjoy. The village people were good to us and supplied us with lots of refreshing provisions.

The evening to remember was when Katarina made her Greek stuffed meat pies. From the start of the meal we discovered something must be amiss as we failed in any attempt to cut into them. We remained as polite as possible while attempting to eat the pies but needed to take care not to break a tooth. During the uncomfortable silence I saw Peter jump up from the table, run out, and shortly come back.

Sitting back down, he pulled out a hammer and chisel and began to attack his meat pie. That was it! We lost all politeness and roared with laughter with Katarina joining in at last. This was a big step for her, as it was obvious she was feeling defensive about her dinner. I'm sure she was disappointed her meat pies didn't turn out like her mother's.

Hitchhiking was the way European youth got from one place to another. This was how we traveled, my first and only experience at this mode of transportation. Two by two we thumbed rides to wherever we were going for the day. I was a lucky girl as Peter was my partner. He was clever at getting us rides with colorful truck drivers.

One of my favorite weekend trips was to Heidelberg. We walked the streets, toured the charming castle high up on the hill, and fell in love with the beautiful Old Bridge over the river Neckar.

I could drive my car but did so only when there was food or luggage that needed to be transported. Sputnik, the name it got dubbed, became invaluable at those times, but it was more fun for me to hitch rides with my peers.

The town of Pfeddersheim and the neighboring town of Worms provided all sorts of reasons to shorten a number of our workdays. On various occasions we got invitations to tour local businesses. One afternoon we quit work early and hopped the train to Worms for a grand tour of the furniture factory. Following the tour we were treated to a tasty meal of traditional German foods. Of course, that included generous helpings of meat and potatoes.

While in Worms we sought out the site where Martin Luther was accused of heresy after posting his Ninety-Five Theses on the door of the Castle Church in Wittenberg. The Edict of Worms in 1521 branded him a heretic at that time. Many changes are obvious in our world since that long-ago day.

One day we visited the milk factory and another day the winery. At the end of the milk factory visit, the samples of milk tasted good and nutritious, but they were not as popular as what came at the end of the winery tour. We found the winery process informative, but the cellar was too cold for our liking. It seemed the lecture down there went on forever.

Things warmed up as we were offered tasting glasses of wine at the conclusion of our tour. No one seemed to care about the ages of the young people in our group, I noticed. After finishing the one glass, there was more for the taking from the numerous bottles on the table. For the European youth it all seemed quite natural—nothing special—with no one even thinking of overdrinking.

To our surprise one Saturday morning, Swiss Else and Dutch Anton announced their engagement. They'd met in a work Ccmp three years before and wanted to make their engagement official at camp. The whole day became special, beginning with fresh peaches for breakfast and followed by an official ring ceremony. Lots of speeches and champagne! They treated us to a boat trip on the Rhine River from St. Goar to Bingen. The river cruise took us by the legendary Lorelei Rock that juts up from the narrowest spot on the river and seems to make an eerie murmuring echoing sound.

While on the boat trip I flinched as an obnoxious American family paraded around as though they were the only ones on deck. The seated father was reading in a loud overpowering voice from the tour book. The kids were racing around from one spot to another with the mother yelling at them to stop. There was no way to avoid their intrusion.

The term "Ugly American" came to mind as I saw them through the eyes of our group. My companions, along with many other travelers, never complained. They continued to quietly enjoy each other and the sights as appropriately as they possible could while attempting to ignore the distraction. As for me, I was busy pretending I wasn't an American.

On the job site our local supervisors treated us like family, creating special nights with delicious tortes and other elaborate desserts for our indulgence. Lack of knowing all the languages didn't stand in our way of understanding and enjoying each other. We became a close-knit group that loved our time together.

Each night was turned into special programs and singing fests, many nights around a camp fire. It was our good fortune that Dick had brought his guitar. He accompanied our love for singing all the old camp songs. Anyone who could remember a favorite would teach it to the group. "Kum Ba Yah," "Vive L'Amour," "Sarasponda," "Michael Finnegan," "Tell Me Why," and all the familiar rounds were loved by all of us and sung over and over.

On two nights I was corralled into showing slides of my time in Jordan. I was happy to share with them the work I'd done with the people of Palestine and tell them more about their plight of wanting to return to their homes.

When the six weeks wound down it was hard to say good-bye, cheerio, auf wiedershen, au revoir, dag, and yasou. Knowing I'd be touring in Europe and having made promises to stop and see new friends made it easier.

Letters were coming from Jericho. Reading them made me uneasy, as for the present I was attempting to put that chapter of life out of my mind. After the letter I'd written Hanna I thought the saga would be over, but it seemed he was still insistent.

Now I was in a different world and not ready to deal with how I felt about what had gone on previously. When a letter came I gave it a quick read and then stuck it safely in the bottom of my suitcase.

*This is my private story. I'm not sharing the confusion I feel right now with my fellow campers. With so much going on around me, I want to live only in the present. There will be a time later to react and face my true feelings.*

*Jericho*
*16 July '59*

*My darling Myrna,*

*I have your letter which to be candid was a shock. My first real lesson in this life, a cruel one, has been given to me by you. I can't tell you everything I feel because it is too much, and because I don't really care about words. I can easily tell you my feeling when my arms are around you for then you may know what I feel. You have proved in your letter that you are a practical girl and I am afraid what you have done the right thing in the circumstances, but I tell you, and I am sure of this, we shall see each other in future, in the near future, I hope.*

*Believe me, Myrna, we shall meet again in spite of every thing, in spite of my people, your people, in spite of even your head and mine, in spite of everything and I hope that you will help me. Is it silly of me to still think of you: It's so strange after all this long time; you remain the same in my mind. So sweet, so grave and gay in one mood, so high—hot-tempered—so hotheaded, and good-hearted.*

*Darling, I think of you always and especially now because the moon is young exactly as she was when we first kissed!!!*

*I still feel the warmth of your lips. I still feel your breath on my face. I even imagine you are close to me, and I keep my eyes closed to prolong the feeling, because when I open them I find alas that I am alone. Is this not cruel of fate? Why do we lose these days? When we should have been together all the time?*

*Write to me my sweetheart. Write soon and for heaven sake, write a long, long, long, letter.*

*God bless you Myrna, and may we soon be together again for eternity.*

*Yours*
*Hanna XXX*

*P.S. I saw your picture with many friends in Jericho. They asked me if I have one or not, but my answer was, her picture is always printed in my heart. Is that true?*

*P. P. S. I am waiting your answer, and I hope I will receive it very soon. Please tell me if you have heard or read something about Elizabeth Baret Browning, especially her top: Relive how much I love thee.*

*Jericho*
*27 July '59*

*My dearest Myrna,*

*This is the second letter I write to you without getting any letter from you. But I am still thinking that it is very difficult to me to finish very quickly all the things I want to say it.*

*Someday I told you that it is very difficult to the Arab man to forget very quickly if he fall in love with a woman, any woman in the world especially the American one. So I am still as you left me. I don't know really if you arrived Germany or not, but anyway I am waiting your letter and I hope I will get it before I leave Jordan to Egypt. I can't honey wasting my time, so I preferred to go to Egypt this year till I hear from you that you are ready to accept me as a husband in Iowa. I am still considered you really my Mrs. Farraj.*

*Tomorrow I want to go to Jerusalem to see Tina to ask her about you and about the best thing that I can do it now. I can't change my feelings towards you. Many and many tried to do that but all of them failed to change any little feeling about you or to stand in my way.*

*Darling Myrna,*

*Is it silly of me to still keeping this feeling about you? I think no, because I love you, and you love me. Don't try please to lie on yourself and try to persuade your heart that you must forget me. Please, and please tell me everything about you, about your family, and about your life in Germany.*

*I am always asking about the shortest way that would help me to land in Iowa very quickly. All my family now are okay, especially my brother Dr. Samir. He is ready to help me as possible as he can. Let me now finish my letter hoping that you will write very soon to me. God bless you, write me soon.*

*Yours always*
*Hanna Farraj XXXXX*
*Jericho, Jordan*

*Have you heard any new records? Please try to hear MY HEART IS SINGING song by Paul Anka especially when he said: Darling, I love you so much.*

*Amman*
*8 August '59*

*My dearest Myrna,*

*While I write this letter to you, I am still thinking between myself and between me about my future and about you. Now I decided to leave Jordan to Cairo to continue my studies this year and I hope in the second year I will be in the states.*

*I don't know if you forgot me, or you still think about me, because I didn't get any letter from you till now. So I can't guess what is your true feeling towards me now and tomorrow and in the future.*

*About me, I am still as you left me in Jericho, but now I am spending such days in Amman near Dr. Samir. We still, me and Samir talk about you, and about your work and about the time that we spent it in Jordan. Samir said, that if you still loving her I am ready to send you to U. S. A. to marry there.*

*Darling Myrna, I met Tina in Jerusalem and I asked her about you, but she said that she did not get any message from you yet, only a card you send it while you still in your lovely trip. I received a card from Agnes in occasion of her marriage, and I hope some day we will send to all our friends the same card when I land in Iowa near you.*

*I shall write to you when I arrive Cairo and I hope that you will write me soon.*

*God bless you, and I am always*

*Yours*
*XXX*
*H. Farraj*
*Jericho, Jordan*

H. Farraj
20/8/59
Jericho, Jordan

My dearest Myrna,

I cannot feel happy again until I get the answer of my letters. I had wrote to you about five letters and till now I didn't get any letter from you. I don't know what is the reason yet, but I don't blame you.

I loved you so deeply and wanted you forever and ever. But when I met you last time in my house, I looked in your face and tried to see whether you were sincere and whether you had true love for me, but I can't carry in my heart anything against you because you are my angel, my beloved, and because I love you so I am ready to fight against the world to bring you beside me, and then I can't utter a word except to kiss you and hold you.

Now I finished everything concerning my traveling to the United States as a student to Washington State. And I hope you still on your promise. I am considering you as Mrs. Farraj and when I'll be in the states I am going to land in Iowa like a bomb. Are you ready to hold it?

My Darling, after a week I will leave Jordan to Cairo to study this year in Egypt, and I hope you will write me soon. I am always in need for your love Myrna. So please write me soon on this address:

Hanna Farraj
74 Cobessy Street
Daher,
Cairo

*I am waiting your answer very soon. God bless you and re-member always*

*Yours,*
*H. Farraj*
*XXXX*
*XXX*

# 23

# TOURING EUROPE

FOLLOWING MY EXHILARATING six weeks of camp I collected three American girls who were working in Europe and willing to tour with me for a few weeks. Taking Tinika with me, I picked up each girl at different spots along the way and dropped Tinika at the nearest point to her home in Holland, promising I'd be back to see her later.

Doreen, Mary, Sarah, and I were off to Brussels, where the World Fair had been the year before. The Atomium, a giant model of a cell with its crystals, was the only thing left standing from the fair. We discovered that the top of the Atomium was a great place from which to see all of Brussels.

It didn't take us long to learn that Belgium produced marvelous chocolates. *So yummy and good!* It wasn't just the delicious chocolate we fell in love with, but we discovered their waffles were fantastic. We found them so exquisite we ended up having them for breakfast, yes, but also for dinner as well.

It was late August when we arrived in Paris. As we were forewarned, we found that most Parisians were off on holiday. The beautiful city was left for the tourists. Just like everyone else we visited all the usual, touristy Paris spots. But for me the most memorable experience in Paris was getting stuck in lanes of the giant traffic circles.

Once I entered into a circle with its heavy traffic going at top speed, my little VW wasn't able to move over to the lane I needed to be in to exit onto our preferred street. There was just too much traffic! Cars were popping in at rapid succession from the many side streets. All this caused us to keep going around again and again until at last I'd manage to find an opening to exit onto the right street.

It became a joke: "It's our second time around, Myrna!"

"Third time around! Third time's a charm!"

"How many rounds did we make this time?"

It seemed I didn't do this once, but every time we had to go through a roundabout it was as difficult for me to handle as the time before. The hardest one by far to navigate was the huge Arc de Triomphe circle. Years later I saw they added traffic lights to all the circles, which had to make the job much easier and less frustrating. Without a doubt, it slowed down the traffic.

I was looking forward to traveling through the Black Forest of Germany to the French Alsace countryside, where relatives lived in a small village named Soppe le-Bas. This is where my Great Grandfather Michael Martin had been born and left at age twenty-two to find his way to Iowa and to marry young Salome Kempf. Grandmother Emma, his daughter, and Aunt Orpha had kept correspondence with Great Grandpa's brother's family all these many years.

Before I left the States they'd encouraged me, "No American relative has done this, Myrna. We're counting on you. We have all the family names and where they live. If you find Grandpa Martin's birth village and the cousins in Alsace, that will make us happier than anything else. You can do it!"

And so I had my job cut out for me: finding the small village and the houses of my relatives. All would have worked out as planned, except we ran out of gas on our way through the Black Forest. I knew we were getting low in petrol, but we had gone many kilometers without a village in sight and no chance to fill up.

When Sputnik drew her last breath there was no indication of how far ahead it would be before we'd find a gas station. Together we made the decision that Mary and I would stay with the car while Doreen and Sarah hitchhiked to the next village to collect a tankard of petrol. That decision was based on the fact that Doreen and Sarah were best at speaking German and French. It was obvious that catching a ride might be a major problem as there was almost no traffic on the road. In fact we hadn't seen another car for quite some time.

To our relief, just about the time we were getting very discouraged, a lovely couple came along to save the day. They lived in the next village, took Doreen and Sarah with them to purchase petrol, and delivered them back to us with the needed fuel. It was our good fortune that running out of gas only delayed us a couple of hours, although it had given me some needless worry.

Upon arriving in Soppe le-Bas and locating my relatives' house, we received a warm welcoming from Cousin Rosalie. She escorted us up the mountain to the family vineyards where her husband Vincent Martin and their son, Jean Pierre, were working the ground around their grape vines with their prize oxen. Here the people lived in the village, with their land away from their houses, not like the farms in Iowa where we lived on our land, away from our neighbors.

*My Paternal Relatives in Alsace*

The cousins greeted us with great enthusiasm. After proudly introducing us to the prize oxen and showing us the grape crop on the vines, they took us around to visit relatives, both in Soppe le-Bas and nearby villages. We got to see the house of my great grandfather's birth and the Catholic church where he was baptized as a baby. We walked the streets and met the families out strolling for their evening walks, families whose kinsmen grew up with my great grandpa.

The relatives lived in beautiful country homes where the house and barn were both under one long roof. It was all very clean and tidy with lovely flowers everywhere. We were treated in grand style. That meant we got served the local sauerkraut and pork dish with all the trimmings. We drank the family wine and had the traditional cheese as the last course of every meal. After a couple of nights with them, we were sent off with a bottle of spirits from their vineyard for my parents. I still have the bottle to this day, empty now of course.

Volkswagens are rather small, with very little trunk space. We were four girls, each with luggage, and of course we still had my two oversized suitcases that I'd dragged with me from Jordan. I'd bought a luggage carrier for the top of my car, and that's where the two big ones were stored.

Traveling the German autobahn was a harrowing experience, as there was no speed limit and the traffic was heavy. One extra-windy day while on the busy highway, an incredible event occurred. It was late afternoon, and the bright sun was behind us. I was amused to notice that I could see the shadow of our car racing ahead and a little to the left of us. Just as I was making a joking remark about that fact, in the shadow my eyes caught the sight of my two large suitcases flying off the top of the car.

With the heavy congested traffic it took me some time to get over to the right lane and pull off the road. In an instant Sarah and I were out of the car and running pell-mell back one-fourth kilometer, more or less, to the spot where cars were swerving in reckless fashion to avoid hitting my two oversized suitcases.

I was sure they might've burst open and we'd find the contents strewn all over the road, but it was my good fortune they'd remained closed. With our adrenalin kicking in we waved our arms wildly and rushed out to pull them to the side of the autobahn.

Not until everything was safely back where it belonged did we fully understand the extent of our danger. "Thank God we're safe!"

Following our adventure it didn't take us long to stop and buy some straps to tie the cases down: a simple detail that should've happened from the beginning, of course.

Switzerland was beautiful, with the majestic Alps rising upward without end, it seemed. This was the view we saw in every direction we turned. To our eyes the landscape looked neat and perfect. We took chair lifts up the Matterhorn where we froze ourselves, hiked in the mountains until we developed blisters, and got in on some lovely folk dancing and singing with Alpine horn blowing.

Since we never made plans ahead we had trouble finding lodging on more than one occasion. We'd spend time going from place to place until something available appeared. This meant we ended up in some indescribable places: like the night that from our bedroom we needed to walk through an occupied second bedroom to get to the toilet. *This is an awkward embarrassment! At least we're in the far bedroom.* Such experiences only added to our amusing adventures. More often then not we hunted for the youth hostels, as they offered the cheapest beds and were clean and comfortable.

\*\*\*

It was the bicycles! Driving in Amsterdam was worse than driving in Paris, I soon discovered. They came in droves. The street corners had no traffic lights or stop signs but were the basic right-of-way corners. That meant whoever was on your right could go first, and that included bicycles. Who would've thought that bicycles could be so intimidating? In spite of my uneasiness while driving, even I was impressed that I did a fine job and had no problems.

In Amsterdam I became so brave behind the wheel that one night I tackled driving us through the red-light district. We found it fascinating to see the girls in the windows in their provocative poses. At the same time it was sad. Did they want to be there? What's going to happen to them next in their lives? Business looked good, as we noted the busy street full of lonesome-looking men. It was evident some were out to find escorts.

After two full weeks of touring, my life slowed down as I spent a week in Holland where Mary worked and shared her room with me. Now I had time to read in depth the four letters Hanna sent me while at camp, which I had stuck in the bottom of my suitcase.

Reading the letters was quite overwhelming. I didn't know what to think. He just didn't give up! The letters were disconcerting for me. I didn't know how to react. I thought it would be over. I had put off writing back to him for too long. It was time for me to answer. But what should I say? Sentiments were swirling in my head.

*I thought the letter I wrote Hanna would give him a way out, and it would be ended. But he sounds just as determined as ever to make it work. I don't see how we can possibly get together.*

*No one has ever showered this much love on me. Can it be for real? Do we really know each other? Dear God, help me! I really don't know how to handle this. I miss him! I long to have it work out, but I don't see how it possibly can happen.*

*I'll write again to let him know he's free to let it end. It must slow down. It's scary and more than I can comprehend. I feel sad! It's true; I love him more than I knew I could love anyone. But where can it go? I'd much rather it stopped now than later be disappointed and hurt even more.*

*14/9/59*

*Dear Hanna,*

*I might as well be frank from the start and tell you that I haven't written because I can't decide what to write. I am quite sure we don't know each other as well as we should before making big decisions.*

*If you are demanding an answer from me now it will have to be NO, as I feel too uncertain about the thing. If you are willing for us to be friends and write and learn more things about each other before we make up our minds, I would be willing and happy for that opportunity.*

*I think you will not like that so much, but Hanna, you must remember you can't force anyone to love. I know because I tried it once.*

*I hope your school is going good and that you are happy there. I have had such a nice summer and have seen so many things. Europe is a very beautiful country. Right now I'm in Holland but will soon go to England and then on the 24th to America by boat. My parents and sister and her husband are meeting me in New York.*

*My car is blue, not black, and has been doing well.*

*My home address is only Parnell, Iowa, U.S.A. if you want to write and tell me what you thought of this letter. I'm sorry it sounds so cold. I think I'm, perhaps, afraid of you.*

*Sincerely, Myrna*

# 24

# BACK TO AMERICA

DELIGHTFUL THINGS HAPPENED during my week in Holland. In addition to catching up with much-needed personal chores, like washing all my clothes and answering friends' letters, I got to visit Dutch native Tobia at her university in Leiden.

Tobia, as a foreign student to the States, had been my college sophomore roommate. She was an exuberant soul with a quirky mind of her own. It was no surprise when I found she met me at the train station and took me on a tour of the university and her club on the crossbar of her bicycle. Riding on her crossbar was in itself a hilarious adventure. I couldn't stop laughing as we wove through the streets, the raw truth being I was scared half to death. I thought we'd topple over at any moment. *Nothing's changed! With Tobia, one never knows what to expect.*

Being a university student in the Netherlands seemed quite different from in America. The students didn't attend classes, just studied on their own. I got the impression it all depended upon how they did on final examinations. It looked to me like they crammed like crazy when a test was near and more or less goofed off the rest of the time.

Luck was with me as Tobia was in one of her goofing-off stages. She entertained me at a Chinese restaurant with friends who were lively and fun. We got along better than we had back in our college sophomore year. It was obvious I had grown up, gained some confidence, and now held my own compared to those days.

Another day Haiji, who'd been one of our camp leaders, gave me a thorough tour of Amsterdam. We walked through the university he attended, went to the art museum that houses all the Rembrandts, and saw the other spots he thought worthwhile. The full day was followed by a dinner he prepared for me in his apartment. He, like Tobia, seemed to be an eternal student.

During the evening, I talked Haiji into going with me to Rotterdam later in the week. A big job was ahead for me, and I knew it would be easier with a native. I needed to take my two oversized suitcases to the Holland American Lines in Rotterdam where they'd be put on the SS *Ryndam*, the ship I'd board later in England. Then I'd drive my Volkswagen to the US liner for its journey to New York. I had come a long way in handling whatever I had to do, but it would be great to have Haiji with me to do the talking. Plus it would be a lot more fun with him.

It was a blessing to have Haiji with me in Rotterdam when I needed to drop my bags and my VW off at the docks. With Sputnik's help, we first spent time seeing the sights of Rotterdam. It all seemed quite industrial compared to Amsterdam, not nearly as interesting.

My most memorable impression of the city came from viewing the massive sculpture called *The Destroyed City* by Ossip Zadkine. It boldly represented a person without heart and center and with arms and hands straight up in agony. It was a memorial to the destruction of the center of Rotterdam in 1940 during World War II.

Haiji told me a sweet story about a little boy who was riding behind his father on a bicycle and said to him, "Papa, I wish you had a hole like the sculpture so I could see where we're going."

After touring Rotterdam, we said bon voyage to Sputnik, and Haiji caught the train back to Amsterdam. I went to a movie to fill time before once more going down to the pier. Mary, who was going on holiday with me in England, met me, and we embarked on the late night boat across the English Channel into London. Although the water was rough, it was an easy crossing. We crawled into bunk beds, fell fast asleep, and when we woke we were in England.

The two of us gained some culture during our week of touring London. We took in Old Vic Company's Shakespearian *As You Like It*. We loved our standing-room-only tickets for *My Fair Lady* at Drury Lane. In spite of SRO, or because of it, we had excellent viewing with no one in front of us. We couldn't have asked for better seats than where we were ushered to sit on a front aisle step. Along with hitting all the usual London tourist sites, we ended the week by attending a BBC concert at the Royal Albert Hall. For us it was a smashing week in London Town.

When the time came for the S.S. *Ryndam* to leave port, I headed down to Southampton to board the ship to cross the Atlantic. I was in a cabin for four with the bathroom down the passageway. This was one voyage that for me didn't prove pleasant. On the second day we hit hurricane waters and the rough seas pitched the boat both day and night. Everyone, including the Captain the rumor had it, turned green with seasickness.

On this voyage I ended up spending a couple of days in the loo, hanging on to a bar, as I couldn't stop the heaves. What a relief to finally see the Statue of Liberty and know I would soon be back on American soil. I learned with a vengeance what it meant to be seasick, something I had avoided until this voyage.

When my ship arrived, my parents, my sister, and her husband were there to meet me. My two years abroad faded into what seemed no time at all as I got caught up on life in the States. Our plan was that one of them would drive with me back to Iowa. To our great disappointment we found that the longshoremen were on strike, and nothing was happening at the docks. So, no Sputnik!

My family brought a letter from Hanna that he'd sent to my home address. Now I'd find out his reaction to my second appeal that we needed to let this whole idea cool.

*I'm pleasantly impressed. Finally he is making sense. He's willing to forget the marriage idea and write as friends. I'm looking forward to that. There's no doubt I love him. He still is the best thing in my life. Maybe God will find a way for us to get together somehow, someday.*

My family and I spent a week visiting around the area, hoping that the longshoremen would end the strike and I could get my car. But it didn't happen! And they had to head back to their responsibilities in Iowa. My sister Marilyn needed to care for her young children—Bonnie, David, Jean, and Douglas—the nieces and nephews I was eager to see after two years. I hoped they'd remember me.

Since I couldn't leave without my car, I had to stay on. It was an unpleasant experience because as the time extended, my money supply ran lower and lower. I spent my time walking the streets, finding museums and other spots to visit that didn't require an admission fee. There was no choice but to eat fewer meals and keep moving down to cheaper lodging.

That put me in some rather seedy spots with quite thin walls. I'd rather not have known every conversation between disputing couples and hear every activity of the lovers in the room next to mine. I learned some people's lives must be miserable, and some people have very noisy rendezvouses. I guess we can say that I extended my education.

After another long, frustrating week the longshoremen strike was resolved at last, and I could go down to the docks and collect Sputnik. I found the spot where my car was unloaded and claimed it but still needed to appear at the nearby US Customs office to pay import duty. There the man in charge, with paper in hand, announced my payment. To my startled ears it sounded like an exorbitant amount of money.

For the last two years I'd remained strong no matter what challenges came my way. Numerous times I felt inner anxiety but had always managed to put on a positive front and get through it. But at this news I became completely distraught. I burst into tears and blurted out, "But I only have forty-five dollars left."

I tried to pull myself together as the man in charge excused himself and went back into the inner office. How was I ever going to handle this latest calamity in my life? With not enough money to pay the customs duty, and then more money needed to drive back to Iowa, I was in a bind.

Not getting anywhere with thinking of a solution, I awoke to the realization that the customs officer had appeared again. Without saying a word he handed me a new slip of paper. Glancing down at it I was amazed to see that it now stated I owed thirty-five dollars.

It meant that after paying the customs duty I had enough money for gas and toll fare for the thousand-mile trip home. It didn't leave me any money for food, just a ten-cent coffee every now and then to make sure I stayed awake. This was what life was like before credit cards, ATM machines, and cell phones. *Thank you, God, for compassionate longshoremen customs officers.*

Arriving back home in Iowa, I was kept busy giving talks and showing my slide pictures about my experiences in the Middle East. I was feeling very nostalgic about the people I'd left behind in Jordan, missing them more than I ever would have imagined.

Letters were going back and forth between Hanna and me. My daily prayers: *God, control my life. What is to happen? This is too much for me. Let it be your will. I put it in your hands.*

*Cairo*
*27 of September '59*

My dearest Myrna,

Last night I received your first letter to me. I expected not your letter to be so cold as it is.

I was surprised when I read that you are afraid of me. Why Myrna? Is there anything in mine, which made you afraid of me? But I don't think so. I think you are afraid to say again that you love me. You whispered to me before that you loved me!!

Anyway Myrna I like to be a friend to you while I am here alone in Cairo. But you must know something that my love to you shall never stop even if you are so far away of me.

Before I came here I told my brother that I am still goes so deeply in your love, but he advised me not even to think of you, because he learned the British and the American girl very well, and I think that he was right.

I am sure Myrna that I shall come to the states next September to Washington State in Puget Sound University. I have many friends there, especially Dr. Tom Olinger, who is living now in Bremerton. He promised me to bring me to the states only to continue my studies.

I am not asking you now for marriage Myrna. I wish you the happy life in the future, and I will be very happy to see you in the states again to prove to you that I loved you only for yourself and not for any other thing.

I wish you good luck honey, and I hope that you will write me soon.

*My best regards to your family.*
*Yours*
*H. Farraj*
*74 Cabessy Street*
*Cairo, Egypt*

*P.S.*
*I am very sorry if I cause a trouble to you with your family, but I hope you will explain to them every thing about our friendship.*

*Hanna*

*(Postmarked New York, October 9, '59)*

*Dearest Hanna,*

*I was happy to have the letter from you. My parents brought it along to New York City when they came to get me. I'm having trouble now because I can't get my car off a freighter ship because of the Dock strikes in New York. I have to wait here and I'm getting anxious to get home to Iowa.*

*It was a very nice letter that you wrote and I remembered you and the things we said to each other and planned. And I wished I could see you again—you don't know how hard it was for me to leave Jordan without seeing you. I was so very mixed up.*

*I hope you can fulfill your plans to come to the U.S. next year. If you could come and see how you like it here—then maybe you would see if you still feel the same about me.*

*Why don't you tell me how you like school? Is Tony there too? What are you taking this year?*

*I'll probably look for a job sometime soon. My family is well.*

*I've been thinking of you a lot since I'm home, wondering how you might like it here and wishing I could see you again.*

*With love,*
*Myrna*

*October 22, 1959*

*Dearest Hanna,*

*I've missed hearing from you for sometime. I'm wondering if you are well and happy. Perhaps you are very busy—studying hard, or do you go to lots of parties? You like parties, I remember.*

*I've been home now for some days (about a week.) It's good to be home but I miss Jordan a lot and my Arab friends. People are asking me to talk about Jordan and show my pictures. I want to do that because so many people don't understand correctly about Jordan and Israel, etc. and I want to tell them so they'll know.*

*Tonight I went to my sister's house. She is married and has 4 children—full of lots of life. They seem so much bigger than when I left 2 years ago so I must learn to know them over again.*

*My father is well, but my mother is not so good. She must have an operation. She has gallstones. I don't know what they are in Arabic.*

*I'm afraid I'll forget all the Arabic that I did know. I wish I had someone to talk to.*

*I got my pictures developed. Remember the one Tony took of you and me at Ramallah. (I forget the name of the place.) It is nice I think. Perhaps I can get a print made and send it to you. Do you have any pictures of yourself to give me?*

*What are you studying this year? Do you like school? Is Tony there? How are your mother and father and Samira? I'm wondering what your mother thought of me that last day when I came with Mr. and Mrs. Lehman to your house. I was so unhappy! I still am.*

*Did I tell you about my Volkswagen? It's blue—rather a nice color and I like it a lot. My father has a big Buick, but he likes it very much too. I have to get a job now and pay for it. I had to drive alone from New York City to Iowa. It's over 1000 mile. It took me about 23 hours. Sure would have liked to have someone with me!!*

*Don't study too hard—(or should I say don't go to too many parties.) And write me again sometime. I enjoy your letters and promise to answer. I like you lots, and think about you much!*

*With love to my Arabian,*
*Yours, Myrna*

*Cairo*
*31 of October '59*

*Darling Myrna,*

*Yesterday I was delightful to receive your fine letter. Thank you for it and some of the details of your life and family.*

*In the 20th of this month I answered your lst letter, so I think you did not receive it yet, but anyway here I write you again because I like to write you always.*

*Kiss, you can't imagine how much I love you and how much I respect my love to you, and here in your last letter you talked about parties and enjoyments. First of all I want to say that if "Venus" herself came to me and say that she loves me I will dismiss her, because of you and of your love. I told you that you was my first love and my last one, so don't try to think that Hanna is a young man, and he is going to leave you some day. I'll never, never, and never. I love you and I am waiting the moment in which we can make our marriage. And here I want to say again to tell your parents that if all the Jordanian people stand against me, I will never change my mind towards you.*

*Darling, I don't know what to do exactly to come to the United States, but I know one way which is the shortest way, to get the acceptance from any university in your state, and then I will be in need for a person who can make a "guarantee" to me in the U.S.A. because I can't bring with me much money as the embassy requested. Because I don't want to learn in the university but to stay with my beloved working with her and helping each other. So please tell me everything about this point.*

*I will be very happy to have your picture very soon and in my next letter I am going to send some pictures of me.*

*The school is good, and I don't like to study hard, and to go to too many parties because I fed up since a long time.*

*My family asked me if Myrna write to you or not, but I answered them that both of us is still on our promise.*

*So long dearest, and God bless you. My best wishes to your parents and to your sister and her husband.*

*Yours forever*
*Hanna XXX*

*P.S. I am studying now something about the Protestant church and I think that after a couple of week I am going to declare that I am a Protestant.*

*2. P.S. Write me soon and don't forget to send two pictures. One for you, and the other one, which we took it in "Harb Park" in Ramallah.*

*November 19, 1959*

*Dearest Hanna,*

*I hope this finds you well and happy. I am spending much of my time wondering what our future will be and thinking of you and wishing we could have had more time together to talk and enjoy each other.*

*I have been praying to God that he will help us see what is to happen between us and how it can happen. God sees ahead, I know, and we don't,—so I think—really I do, Hanna, that only God can help us.*

*I know nothing to say at the present about a school here in the states. Hanna, I hope you study hard and if you come to the states you continue your studies, because in America there isn't a very interesting future for anyone without a University degree. It is much better if you study something you like and then you can get a good job in that area.*

*I believe I get more homesick for Jordan than I did for the U.S. when I was in Jordan. I think about Jordan and the people there so much. (Maybe I'll have to go back one of these days.)*

*You can't imagine how cold it is! We had snow now for 2 weeks and very cold icy weather. It doesn't bother me because I'm just at home with my mother and father and stay in the house, which is nice and warm. Today I helped my father haul corn in from the fields to unload and put in the corncrib, and got cold.*

*I don't go around and have lots of fun and good times! And I don't believe you don't go to many parties! That's all right—I wouldn't want you not to be as happy as you can. (Even if I do get a little jealous thinking of you meeting lots of chic Egypt girls!)*

*Yours with love,*
*Myrna*

*P.S. I don't have reprints of pictures as yet.*

*P.S. People are always asking me to talk and show pictures about my work in Jordan. I hate to talk in public but sometimes they give me money so it isn't so bad. HA! One ladies group gave me a bed sheet and 2 pillowcases for my future home. ??*

*Cairo*
*30 Nov. '59*

*Dearest Love,*

 *I received your lovely letter. I was happy to hear from you soon.*

 *Yesterday I finished my examination and I hope that I will get good result for this term.*

 *I am really happy for your truly and frankly talking in your letter, but there is one point I admired about it, or maybe I did not understood what does it mean.*

 *You said that I am going to fail in the states if I didn't work hard and I must study hard here to get a good transcript.*

 *But I don't know. Do you mean that I must work hard to finish my five years studies here? Or what——Do you want me to wait all that time. Really I can't——I can't darling wait all that time without seeing you. I do my best here to come to the states, and have you demand from me to study hard that may I be something in your country.*

 *I can't do anything now till I finish this year. Then I can persuade my family to come to the states to continue my study, and in that time we can prepare ourselves to marry. If it is so hard to me to carry all the responsibilities as a husband, and to study, I am going to leave the university to work beside you so we may live good.*

 *The weather here is so good and gentle and till now we haven't rains. I hope that some day we will spend some of our honeymoon here beside the Nile.*

 *How are your parents, especially your mother? What she is going to do for the gallstones? First she going to make an operation or what? I hope that she will cure very soon.*

 *Also what about your sister? Is she near to your home? I think you enjoy yourself by playing with her kids...or what!!!*

*Here I am sending to you my last picture with my cousin. It is the first year to him here in Cairo. I think I seem so sad in it!!! I hope in your next letter you will send your picture.*

*And now let me say good-bye and till the next letter,*

*With love to my American,*

*Hanna*
*XXX*

*January 7th, 1960*

*My dearest,*

*It's 1960—a new year—what it brings to us we don't know now but it is my prayer that in 1960 we find happiness completely. There are a million things about you I don't know and would like to learn. I think of you a lot and I begin to worry every time I don't hear from you for a long time. It seems a long time now.*

*Is it your Greek Orthodox Christmas, I think? Did you spend it in Egypt? With friends, I hope.*

*This picture is the one from Ramallah. You are sad on it, too. I wish I could see your smile.*

*I visited Wayne and Agnes in Illinois. It's only a 5-hour drive from my home. I also visited a very dear girl friend of mine in Illinois whose husband just became a Doctor. She has two small children and I like her very much. I told her all about you, and showed her your picture. She said, "He looks as though he has got good character. He has a firm mouth." I said, "He Does!"*

*Agnes and Wayne seem very happy. They live in a little apartment (or flat) in his father's house.*

*I will write again when I hear from you. I keep worrying about you. I'd like to see you so much. I know my life is incomplete without you. Inshallah, someday before very long we can be together. Inshallah!*

*With love to my Arabian Lover and sweetheart,*
*Myrna*

*Jericho,*
*22 January, 1960*

*Darling Myrna,*

*Today I came from Amman after I saw my brother Samir. You know that I came home to Jordan just to put an end to our love with my family. Before we start talking anything, he showed me your letter. He was so astonished to receive it in this week because your letter was dated in the 13th of November '59. But when we looked to the address we guessed that the reason was your wrong address.*

*Now I want to explain everything to you, and I want to give you my last decision in our love.*

*In every letter I wrote to you I told you that you are my first and last love. And I proved to you here in Jordan that my love to you is true and deep in my heart. Before I know you I had many girl friend here in Jordan and also in Egypt. But I think you know the difference between a girl you love her and another just to spend the time with her. But when I know you, everything was changed, my feelings towards girls, my way in life, everything in my personality was changed because I fall in love with you.*

*You heard many things here in Jordan about me, and you know what are they. But I think you have your own opinion about me, and the girl whom she have a strong personality she will never change her mind about a thing she know it well.*

*Tonight I met Hanneh in her house. We talked about you a big talking, and all the members of the MCC here in Jericho are fond to meet me, and I don't know the reason yet. But I think they are going to ask me about the result of our love, so I want to prove to them that our love is Immortal.*

*My brother will write to you very soon, and I hope that you still well as I know you, and I swore to you that you still in my heart till ever. Don't think to marry any American boy for my sake and for the sake of our love.*

*Myrna, I love you——I love you——and I shall love you always till the end of my life.*

*I am going to write to your father very soon, and I hope that he may help us.*

*Till the next letter I wish you good luck, and a happy time.*

*Yours forever,*
*Hanna Farraj*
*XXXXXX*

*P.S. At the end of this month I'll be in Cairo.*

*Sunday eve, Jan. 31, 1960*

*Dearest Hanna,*

*Since I haven't had a letter from you since the one you wrote on November 30th, I keep thinking something's happened. Either, you wrote to me and I didn't get the letter, or you maybe don't want to write anymore??? I can't know. I keep thinking maybe you are ill. It bothers me. It seems so far from Iowa to Cairo, and I long to see you!!*

*One of my girl friends is getting married next Saturday. She is so happy. And I am so lonesome. I seem to spend a lot of time thinking. There are so many things I don't know about you. I keep thinking about those days together in Jordan and I think now that you were right about so many things. I was just so slow to see the truth. Now I see that I admire you so much more than any other man.*

*Some of the things I admire? 1st: Because you have some very definite beliefs and you feel they are worth hardship to get or live. Also something I can't forget, in one letter you said I was in one mood high tempered and hotheaded. When I think that you said at the same time I was hotheaded, that you loved me, I feel so happy I want to cry. Because I am not perfect, so very far from it and if someone can really see what I'm like and still love me, it makes me feel very humble. I feel like doing everything I can for that person all his life.*

*Darling Hanna, I hope you are not ill!! I want to see you so much and I want you to kiss me …*

*Love always and always,*
*Myrna XXX*

*Did you get the 2 letters I sent you? The one in December and the other in January?*

*Monday Feb 1, 1960*

*Darling Myrna,*

*You will be very surprised when I tell you that I am writing this letter to you while I am flying from Amman to Beirut and then to Cairo.*

*Do you know what's the last talking with my brother in the airport was? I love Myrna and I can't stay away from her. But tell now I don't know what is the best thing I must do in Cairo to come to you. I had met Hanneh many times in Jericho. She is waiting your letters to her and I think she is going to go to the states in June 1960 with Sophy Farran.*

*Darling,*

*Let us help each other to reach the aim safely, and I hope that we will arrive very soon. I had sent a letter to your father just to tell him our story of love.*

*I hope you will write me soon, telling me everything.*

*With all my love,*
*Yours forever*
*Hanna Farraj*

*Cairo*
*4th Feb. 1960*

*Dearest Myrna,*

*Last night I arrived Cairo from Beirut. When I reached the home I took your lovely letter contains our picture. It was surprise for me seeing myself very sad. But I think it was my right feelings that some day I will loose you.*

*Here I want to say for you that I can't wait all this time. I am going to be mad. I feel sadness when I look to your picture, which I brought with me from Jordan. Every time, and every moment I remember you, and I think the best thing we do it to find a salve to our story of love.*

*Today I met an American friend to me and I told him everything about us and we discussed many things. But at last we found that the best thing and the shortest way is: I go to "Italy" and you come there, and then we can get married so easy.*

*So now I am waiting your answer very soon, and I prefer to start our plan in this month. You can take permission from the school and so I, just ten days if you come by the airplane. We must do a sacrifice to complete our love, and to show all the world that we were not kidding. To do the same thing as Agnes and Wayne, and before them many lovers.*

*You know that I changed all my plans in life because of you, and I can't wait now without knowing the end of our love. If you are sure of yourself you must come———Don't be a hesitating girl. You are over-age and you know what is good and what is bad.*

*Now you mustn't look to any other thing in life. We must put an end of our love. You may be angry on me because I can't wait, but if you are in my position you will never wait. I have now a little amount of money, about 50 pounds, which could be enough to let me reach ROME and to wait you tell you come. There we can make everything without any trouble, and when we finish the* wedding you go back to U.S.A. and I return to Jordan waiting your sign to leave.

I am waiting your answer. Don't be late. My best wishes to your parents, especially your mother. I heard that she made an operation to get out the gallstones.

With all my love to my future wife...

Yours forever
Hanna

P.S I sent a letter to your father. I told him everything about us. I am waiting your answer very soon. Tell me everything about your last decision.

*Feb 7, 1960*
*Parnell, Iowa*

*Dearest Hanna,*

*Tonight we had a long discussion about you and me and what was going to happen. My father received your letter and he wondered about my decision. My father, like other people, feels that if you come to the states you must realize that life in the U.S. is not exactly an easy life and perhaps you wouldn't like it.*

*His strongest feeling and I agree with him on this, is that it would not be wise for you to live and work on the farm. He says it's hard enough for someone who has grown up on the farm to do it because it takes a lot of capital and more and more farming is going into the hands of the big dealers.*

*He would much rather you continued your studies here in the U.S. and then enter something you like, and from what he said I think he would help you.*

*But we don't know at all what you might like or what studies you like best. It makes some difference in the college or University one would go to—for certain studies are better in certain areas in different colleges.*

*Also, I want to say, it need not be in Iowa. But if you could get an acceptance in a good school anywhere I will go with you. I'm not so fond of living in Iowa. Do you think you can transfer your credits easily?*

*My heart is singing tonight, but longing to be with yours. I rather hope your brother writes. My father thinks he should know what your family thinks about it.*

*Oh, Hanna darling. I do love you and pray God will help us meet.*

*Be good, Honey, and happy, and contented until we can be together.*

*With Love and Devotion,*
*Myrna*

*The 10th of Feb, 1960*

*Darling Myrna,*

*Last night I received your lovely letter. I was very surprised to know that you did not receive any letter from me since a long time. I sent three letters to you since I left Cairo. The first one on the 15th of Jan, and at the same time I sent another letter to your father. And on the first of Feb, 1960, I sent a letter to you from Beirut, while I was flying from Amman to Cairo via. Yesterday morning I sent another letter to you.*

*I don't know what is the reason which prevents my letter from reaching you. Maybe the Egyptian Army Control, and maybe from the post office in your city, anyway you must know that in every month I send to you more than two letters.*

*In my last letter I talked about marriage and the shortest way to complete our love so quickly. From my side I want to say that all these days have passed without doing anything concerning marriage. Many of my friends advised me that the best thing to do is to travel to Rome or Beirut both of us and get married there.*

*I want to say that I don't care to my family at all. I told them that no one can change my feelings towards my beloved. You must be sure that our love will be the most effective thing after our marriage. In fact, I want to tell you many things about the future, but I don't want to mention them here in my letter. I want to whisper them in your ears!*

*I have told you nothing concerning my studies, to tell you the truth; I am very perplexed and have not begun yet. Please tell me frankly your last decision whether you are going to send me a cable telling me when and where we are going to meet each other to get married, and in this case I will fly directly with you to the U.S.A., or you will not come, and in this case I can see to my future and studies. Of course, you know my true feelings towards you, darling. I can't sleep day or night in wait of your arrival, and I am not exaggerating when I tell you that your picture haunts me wherever I go, even in my dreams.*

*You know my conditions very well. Had I enough money at present, I would fly immediately to your land. You must know that my father wants me to stay with him in Jordan, and of course you know quite well the love of the parents.*

*I have nothing to do now save to fly on the wings of imagination to your home, and indeed, I do that several times a day and imagine that we are close to each other whispering and kissing. In fact, I want my arms round you, and your head on my heart, and my lips on yours——etc.*

*What a pity to be separated in such a cruel way. How wonderful are dreams!!! But the most wonderful of all is their coming true. You don't know how I suffer my dearest love. You don't know how you have tormented me, but in spite of all hardships, in spite of all obstacles... "Hanna is for Myrna and Myrna is for Hanna."*

*Your Arabian Beloved,*
*Hanna*
*XX*
*X*

*Feb 12th, 1960*

*My dearest Hanna,*

*Sometimes I feel I'm really silly because I just want to write to you so badly and just tell you of my love for you. But never mind, if it's silly the way I feel, then I'm happy just to be silly.*

*Hanna, you don't know me. I feel so unworthy of your love. Sometimes I am so selfish,—and I believe you think I am good and kind—and I hope I can always be. I will be—if someone loves me very much.*

*In one letter to me you referred to Elizabeth Browning's poem on Love. I like it very much, too.*

*"I love thee to the depth, and breadth and height my soul can reach."*

*If only we could be near each other. I want to copy one of Elizabeth B. Browning's poems for you because it speaks my feelings.*

*"If thou must love me, let it be for nought except for love's sake only. Do not say, "I love her for her smile—her look—her way of speaking gently,—for a trick of thought that falls in well with mine, and certes brought a sense of pleasant ease on such a day"—For these things in themselves, Beloved, may be changed, or change for thee,—and love, so wrought, may be unwrought so. Neither love me for thine own dear pity's wiping my cheeks dry,— A creature might forget to weep, who bore thy comfort long, and lose they love thereby! But love me for love's sake, that evermore thou mayest love on, through love's eternity."*

*Isn't it pretty?*

*I hope your cousin will not be offended but I cut your picture off from his and put it in a little frame and stood it by my bed. The only trouble is it causes me to think of you so much and I get lonesome and long to see you that sometimes I think I'd better put it in a drawer. Ever since you sent me the picture I can't contain myself. I'm so eager to be with you. I pray God to keep our hearts pure and help us!!*

*I'll send you this picture so you have one but I wish it was a new one and not one everyone else has. Just remember Hanna darling, when I took that picture I was thinking of you!! (That Saturday morning in Jerusalem and we met just outside after I took it and walked and talked.) How hard it was for us. I was so happy to see you and yet so worried Mrs. Lehman or Mrs. Ruegg would see us and think I had it all planned to meet you. And then Nabeel Jahshan saw us at the Ice Cream place and told everyone!! I can really laugh at that now. The only thing I feel so very very sorry about is that I came to your house that last morning with the Lehmans. They didn't make me do it, but they treated me like I was a bad little girl and needed to be watched every moment night and day and I couldn't stand it. I feel it was very weak of me and I wish a thousand times I did not do it. I remember that day as if I were in a dream. Em Fati knew where I was going and why and she asked me How I could? I told her my heart was like the stone. She got tears in her eyes and said, "Haram, Sitt Myrna, if you love him and he loves you, you must not listen to the people. They always always will talk." But I was weak, and I did what they wanted me to do and left my heart like a stone and went to your house. I was as cold as I could be because I was afraid if I wasn't I'd break down and tell you I didn't mean what I said.*

*Oh Hanna, can you forgive me this?? It's cold in my room and I'm writing this to you in my bed. Your picture is sitting there looking so serious at me. It says you forgive me because love forgives and to me you are love, but that's why I feel so unworthy of your love. But I want to love you and everyday I want to love you more until I'm an old grandmother with false teeth and a hearing aid.*

*My heart is so full tonight. Darling, do you mind if your wife is very sentimental? I'm liable to wake you up in the middle of the night crying or laughing at something that happened between us.*

*Please hurry and write to me. I hunger for any news from you.*

*Love Always and Always and Always,*
*Myrna Marie*

    *P.S. Write to me something in Arabic. My teacher from Amman sent me a Christmas card and wrote a message in Arabic. All I can remember is (Hanna written in Arabic). Is Hanna like this?*

*Feb 16, 1960*

*Dearest Hanna,*

*I just received your letter, the one with the Italy idea. Oh, Darling, what can I say to you. You just tear my heart. If I tell you the idea is impossible you will think I'm again putting you off, and I hate to make your life so sad. As long as I know you are sad I can't be happy. Please believe me when I tell you I think about you constantly and I am anxious to be your wife and after your nice letter to my mother and father and my talk with them I felt much better and was so happy because I felt they would help us.*

*Now however, I have just begun a new job in the testing research department in Iowa City, a town near my home, and I'm going to take another test and then maybe I'll run a big machine and they'd give me more money, but if I stopped even for 10 days I'm sure I'd lose my job. But this job will continue just through June and then I won't have work again. Your school will be out in June also, I think. You will say—she just puts it off and won't marry me in the end. What can I say but that I love you very much—so much I want to sing at the top of my voice and shout to everyone about Hanna, my beloved!!*

*Shall we rather try our best to get you here on a school visa and if impossible I will come to you in July. Do you believe me? Shall my father write to you telling you this is my wish? You tempt me with the idea of meeting sooner. But my parents would feel it would not be wise for me to quit a job I just began and anyway money would be a problem. We will save money if you can come here first, but if we can't I will come to you some way!!*

*I think I do not understand your feelings completely on the need to prove to the world that we love each other. I am happy if we only prove it to each other and it matters not to me what others think—only what you think. I see why you feel the way you do. It is my fault because while I was in Jordan I said I'd marry you and then I said I would not. So now if I say I will, you cannot believe that I mean it until we are married, is that right? This is the one thing I cannot forgive myself. I treated you badly and I want to spend my life making you happy.*

*And so my darling Hanna, you have my love now even though we're many miles apart. Perhaps my love is small and frail but I am waiting for you to teach me more about love, and then our love will become a Masterpiece of Beauty and Truth.*

*Darling, love me forever and don't be sad because I do love you very much, Myrna*

*P.S. Your brother didn't write. I was wishing he did.*

*Monday the 22 of Feb, '60*

*My dearest Hanna,*

*I hope that you are happy, my beloved. It's hard to be happy and content when we are apart. I realize that so very much but I think it is necessary for us to bear it happily. The other night I was reading a story in the Old Testament of the Bible about Jacob. He went into another land and fell in love with Rachel. Rachel's father said he could marry her if he worked for him 7 years. But at the end of 7 years Rachel's father played a trick on Jacob and gave him his older daughter who Jacob didn't love. So then Jacob had to work another 7 years and then he could marry Rachel. Jacob slaved 14 years for the girl he loved. Isn't it a sad story? But they did get married and had 2 sons. True love does reach its fulfillment.*

*We have much snow. It gets very cold in Iowa. Perhaps you won't like it. The houses are warm however. I got stuck in the snow this afternoon and my dad had to push me out with the tractor. They called me and told me not to come to work. I'm not sure why—except maybe a machine broke.*

*I got the letter you registered. Maybe I got all your letters. They just took a long time to come and I got worried.*

*Hanna, I'm so happy. I know sometimes I cry because I wish we could be together so badly. But because I know you love me as you do, I too am a different person from what I was before I met you. Sometimes my friends say to me that I seem so radiant and have a love for everything. I feel like shouting. I DO! He loves me! It makes me a new person, because I, too, love him!! It does seem cruel for us to be apart. Oh Hanna, did I do wrong when I wrote and said I thought we should wait until this summer? I don't want to kill our love. I'd be killing myself. Was it wrong of me? Because I'm just one half a person right now.—waiting to come alive with you near me.*

*I do feel so bad about your parents. I hate to see them feeling sad about you coming to America. By the way—where in Jericho did you get a picture of me? From Hanneh, I suppose? Dear Hanneh—did she tell you about Elias? Also, she told me Mr. Lehman gave everyone a raise but Hanneh, because he said she had too much to do with Hanna Farraj and Myrna's troubles! I felt like writing to Mr. Lehman and telling him I could be responsible for my own affairs. The Lehmans should be arriving in New York soon.*

*I miss you so very much, and I think of you always, always with love, Myrna*

*P.S. I wish your ear were near my lips so I could whisper I Love You! Be good and love me always!!*

*52 Daher Street,*
*flat 17*
*Daher, Cairo*

*7th of March, 1960*

*My dearest love Myrna,*

*How glad I was when I received your letters. I can't exactly express my joy indeed when they were delivered to me. The words, in fact, fail to fulfill the meaning I want to say. Your letters came in a suitable time, I was in bed suffering from a severe touch of flu, but when I touched them, when I read your words I was relieved. They were the medicine. They were my recovery.*

*I am still awake. It is after midnight while I am listening to the radio. Abdel Halim Hafiz is singing one of his lovely songs. He reminds me of love, how much he had suffered because of love. I have translated some of his words and they are a real expression of what I feel.*

*"My darling. I can see you though you are afar——while I am sleepless——alone in this wide gloomy world.*

*Every step while you are absent is a dark night, anxiety, and a new wound in my heart——*

*My sweetheart! I can see you with all my soul, with all my heart, with all my love——*

*Your greetings to me, your tender words in my ears, and your gentle smile, are all in my mind——darling!!*

*Oh darling! I can still see your image in front of me, and the darkness of parting from you is still very deep, for a wounded lover cannot know the end of his sufferings.*

*Oh darling!! If I could, I would stay beside you forever and add a thousand lives to mine so as to enjoy your love."*

*Isn't it a lovely song? Don't say that we are over-sentimental. But oh darling. How cruel you are! How hard your decision is! I'll not see you except next July? I'll count the days, hours, and minutes till you come.*

*I told my parents everything and explained to them what our plan is. They agreed at last. It would take a long time to travel to the states as a student because I have to go to Jordan first. So it would be a waste of time. It is preferable that you should come. For my part, I'll do my best to succeed and after our marriage I can join with any university and complete my studies there.*

*Darling! I am somewhat jealous. I want to know everything concerning you daily. Where you go? Whom you meet? To whom you speak? Don't try to hide anything because I have sent a nightingale to watch you, and tell me everything! Don't look around you. It's invisible.*

*My best wishes to your dear father and my love to your mother and sister. You did not mention anything concerning your beloved mother. What about the gallstone? If she had made an operation or not?*

*Now as I lie in bed, the thoughts crowd in my mind, but I am unable to translate them into words. I wish you were now beside me touching you here and kissing you violently to teach you more about love.*

*And now dearest love, here is a long kiss I send you in my letter; try to find it and tell me next time about its magic effect!*

*Yours forever*
*Hanna*
*XXXX*
*XX*
*X*

*P.S. I forgot to tell you that I have moved to a new flat with my cousin who sends you his complements.*

*My new address is*
*52 Daher Street, flat 17*
*Daher, Cairo*
*Egypt*

*Parnell, Iowa*
*March 20, 1960*

*My very own Hanna,*

*Darling, I sometimes feel I am going to go wild with longing to see you and be beside you. Your letters make me so happy because they let me have just a little more of you to think about and cherish.*

*Sometimes I think I don't know anything about you and I almost become afraid wondering if I am just trying to form you into this person that is so easy to love.*

*Here in America it is probably extra serious but people are always having marriage problems. There are women working where I do and they talk to me about their married lives. If I say anything they will say "you feel that way now—but just wait until you are married 10 years. Etc." Some of them sound like they only live with their husbands because it's too expensive to get a divorce. It just makes my heart sick to hear them. Their husbands drink too much or spend all the money the way they don't like,———or they don't think they discipline the children right or he stays out late at night and then treats them like animals. Some of them must have violent tempers!*

*Then I get afraid and I wonder—does it have to be that way? I think ahead and I wonder—in 10 years will I be nagging you and will you be yelling at me and will we be disagreeing on how to raise our children. And I know I would rather remain single than live the life some live.*

*But I can't conclude it will be this way!! First, I feel marriage was designed by God to be a beautiful thing—where human beings can learn about true love...Yes, a heavenly love...And that love can grow between the man and the woman and multiply to their children and into the world to all they contact and live with.*

*Maybe I don't know how you feel about various specific subjects but somehow I feel confident that our lives are aimed in the same direction. We didn't have much time together in Jordan but I shall never forget the way I felt when I was with you and you talked to me about things. It was wonderful—I never felt so near someone in mind so quickly—although consciously, I tried to resist it—probably because it was too good to believe and I didn't feel I dare trust my feelings for fear they would fade away and I would be left empty. I still can't quite believe you really love me.*

*I have decided where the trouble lies in many American marriages. The woman feels she is equal with the man and they both feel they are equal bosses of each other. I sincerely believe God planned the man to be the 'Head' over the woman and the woman to be submissive to the man. This is what I want to Be! But you remember I can get 'hot-headed', so it may be harder for me sometimes then I now think, and you may have to help me remember my ideal.*

*I'm saying these things because I feel if we are determined to get married then we have got to do everything possible to make a very happy and lovely marriage. And I'm starting right now by considering you as the man I will LOVE, CHERISH, AND OBEY always. Because when I get married it's for always, Hanna. I would never consider a divorce! Really I have no doubt but what our marriage will be completely lovely because I feel we have a deep love and an intelligent understanding. However it seems many get married that feel they are madly in love and it ends in divorce or unhappiness—so I guess it is wise to have a determination to make it successful.*

*Also Hanna, one other thing I may have not made myself clear about. When I talked about you being successful here, I didn't mean successful in the eyes of the world. I'm not interested in much money or prestige at all. I only want to have you happy doing something you can enjoy doing that is worthy of you, because I feel you are special, and far above average so I want you to have a good chance. Please understand me. I certainly don't want to urge you into something you don't want.*

*The song you translated was beautiful. You will sing it to me someday———not so far away.*

*Hanna dearest, I hated to hear you were ill with the flu. I hope you were not too miserable and I'm glad if my letters helped you.*

*That nightingale you sent me is a big nuisance! Everywhere I go he sings in my ear. "HANNA LOVES YOU AND YOU LOVE HANNA" Then he whispers "Why don't you dream about the time you can be with HANNA again?" So, I don't get much done but dream about YOU! ...And wish I was just a little nearer to receive that K I S S...*

*Yours forever,*
*Myrna XXXOOO*

*P.S. Greetings to your cousin. Is he the one in the picture?*

*Cairo*
*12 of April, 1960*

*My dearest love Myrna*
 *Before two days I received your last letter. It took a long time till I received it. I don't know why, but I think from the post office in Cairo.*

 *I was very glad to hear from you everything you think about, but here I want to say, that I don't want you to think about divorce at all. We love each other and I don't want to hurt our love by talking about these things. I assure you darling that we are going to live as the two happiest husband and wife in the world.*

 *I want to tell you that I finish the school in the end of May, so I am going to wait you here in Cairo till the middle of July, because it's so easy for both of us to meet each other in Cairo or Beirut, and then we can do what we want.*

 *I told my family about your coming, and I didn't receive any answer from them till now. But I am waiting a friend of mine to leave Cairo to Jericho to explain to them everything, and I think that you know this friend. His name is George Riad Asaid. His father is the owner of "Mena House Hotel." He told me that he knows you very well and he sends to you his greetings.*

 *I am still dreaming about the moment that we could be with each other touching your hair, and holding you with cruel to prove to you that I don't want to stay one moment far from you. How many kisses do you think I want to kiss you when I meet you? I want to put my lips on yours till the eternity because I am so thirsty... Then I can prove to you that I wanted you so much in this big desert.*

 *Don't wait so much to answer me. I hope that your father and mother are in good health. I wish you the happiness and a lovely future life in the occasion of the Easter, wishing that in the next Easter we shall be sitting with our children.*

*Please write soon. I am hungry for any letter from you.*

*With Love and Devotions,*
*Yours forever*
*Hanna*

*Parnell, Iowa*
*April 24, 1960*

*My darling Hanna,*

*I am always so happy to get a letter from you—but they are never long enough nor do they tell me the things you do and everything else I want to know. And it takes weeks to hear from you. I look every day in hopes there will be a letter from my love.*

*Finally, the snow and winter are past and it is green again and much warmer. Today my girl friend, Faye, and I laid out in the sun in our bathing suits so we would get a suntan. (I realize you probably feel like other Arabs that this is silly, but we like to be brown.) I'm not brown tonight but a bright red, and I feel like I'm on fire. We didn't stay very long, but went fishing in a pond on their farm. All the fish we caught were small so we threw them back in. She has a date tonight and I think she is ashamed of her red face. (I never go on dates because I am waiting for my Arabian lover to come and carry me away. And he never comes and I am so lonesome for him!!)*

*Hanna, I become so perturbed about everything. I am afraid your father will never feel it was right for you to marry me and I suppose my parents would rather I could forget you, but I love you so very very much and I know you love me and it is your life and my life that should be thought of most, I know. Someone said Love is more precious and sweeter when it is difficult to attain. That will be true.*

*I know this has all been very hard for you, and that you are completely changing your life for me, and that you have thought about it and struggled much, and so I hate to say more things to make it harder. I promised you I would come to you if there is no other way and I will—because I also cannot wait to be with my sweetheart.*

*But I'm wondering if it won't be possible for you to get any kind of visa if you had the money. You see, if I come to you it will cost my air passage 2 ways and then you will still need money to come, whereas if you could come we would not need to spend as much money. Also, I suppose, I am a little afraid to come alone to a different land and get married without any women that know me to be with me and help me. Do you understand? But again, I promise I will, then not being able to be with you.*

*I think I shall go to a lawyer and get some legal advice and then maybe I'll have better ideas. Also, Hanna, maybe you don't want to leave your country and come to live here, or maybe you don't want to live in Jordan with an American wife? Or maybe you would rather stay in Jordan a few years and then come to the U.S.? I hate to feel that for the love of me you gave up everything.*

*Oh darling, I know if we could be together it would seem easier. I long for you night and day—everywhere I go I am wishing you were by me, and I could lean over and whisper something in your ear or squeeze your hand or kiss your nose.*

*And someday our dreams will be a reality. Until that time I'm thinking and praying for our love.*

*With all love,*
*Myrna*

*P.S. Maybe my letter was delayed because of Ramadan?*
*P.S. I thought George was working in Kuwait. I remember the song he sang about "I have a girl she calls me Honey,' etc.*

*30th of April, 1960*

*Dearest Hanna,*

*It really isn't time for me to write to you, but I get so lonely for you and I want to have you close and talk to you, but you aren't here so I feel I will write you a love letter instead.*

*I think about you so much and am most concerned that you are well and happy. With all the troubles all over the world I only pray God allows us to be together safely soon.*

*This is while I'm in bed once more. I hope you can read it. I think of you all through the day, but at night when I go to bed you are most in my thoughts. I wish I were with you. I think that when it is 11:00 P.M. at night here, it is 5 o'clock in the morning, so when I go to sleep you have been sleeping for some time (at least I believe you should be.) I wish you would tell me of everything you do because I get most jealous thinking of the people you are with and talk to. What do you study? etc? etc?*

*Tomorrow I am going to play tennis with my girl friend Faye and her 2 brothers. I am not good but I enjoy tennis. My mother invited some people for dinner so I have to be here.*

*You remember Leron? He came and talked to you one morning. He wrote to me to tell me he is engaged and hopes to get married this summer.*

*I am so happy to know you love me, Hanna. Today my girl friend Faye was all disturbed because she has 2 boy friends and she doesn't know which one really loves her or which one she loves. I told her I wish Hanna were here to explain things. I had never been loved before you came into my life, Hanna and what is the most wonderful part is that you love me just as I am. I hope I can always love you the way you deserve to be loved.*

*Darling, I am returning that long kiss you sent me. It says that I am yours, you are my DESIRE, my HOPE, my JOY, my ONLY LOVE, my COMFORT, my PASSION, my HEARTBEAT, my*

*BREAD, DEVOTION, INSPIRATION, and only reason for liv-
ing. Please accept it.*

*I don't like to sign my name. I want to go through life with
you, never signing off or finishing something because if I close the
letter it is as though I have stopped a part of my attention to you.*

*If you understand this you are marvelous. I often think your
letters are neater and written in better English than mine. I think
you are pretty wonderful, my lover!!*

*From your silly American girl who is Crazy for you,*
*XXXXXXXXXX*
*XX*
*X*
*Myrna*

*Cairo*
*1st of May 1960*

*My dearest love Myrna,*

*A long month passed without receiving any letter from you. I don't know why—although I wrote to you three letters through this month and I didn't receive any answer.*

*I don't know if there is something new in your life, but I am sure that you will never change your promise to me. I am building my life now on one thing—that I am going to marry the girl whom I loved and admired. I told my family that I'll never come back to Jordan if I didn't marry you, and here I say it again to you that I will never marry any girl in the world if I did not marry you!!! I am going to wander in this wide world as a mad Jordanian Lover till I die.*

*Darling, don't forget that July is so near. Don't try to postpone your promise, I want you——I am in need of you, your warm lips is still on mine. I am still thirsty for the lovely juice that I produce it from your nice lips.*

*My examinations after twenty days. In every page I am reading the story of our love. I don't know if I am going to succeed or not, but I hope that I shall succeed in my love and studies.*

*My best regards to your family.*

*Yours forever*
*Hanna Farraj*

*I am waiting your answer very soon.*

*Cairo*
*17th of May, 1960*

*Dearest Love,*

*I received you last three letters in 10 days time. You will excuse me if you did not receive any answer regularly. The Post delivery is not regulated, and you will be surprised when I tell you that I received two letters at a time.*

*Darling, I long for the day when I can call you Dear Kiss and have a kiss after another! One would be very long one, it will be devoted to your warm lips. Another one, I will keep for your rosy checks. A third and the most affectionate I am not going to tell you where. Can you guess?*

*Oh darling! I count the days, the hours, and the minutes. It's the first of June, our glorious day. The day when we shall meet, the day when we shall see each other, the day when we shall begin a new page of the truest and perfect love!!*

*You asked whether you would come by plane or on board the ship. I think it is better to come by plane; the voyage on board the ship will be very lonesome and nerve racking. So it is preferable to reserve a round trip passage. You know quite well that it would be impossible for me to leave with you until you finish papers.*

*Don't worry much about the cost of your staying with me. You know well the true Arab blood runs in my veins, and it would be a shame for me to let you spend a penny during your stay. So don't worry about it.*

*As for my relatives, don't care much, as I have prepared everything and convinced them that I cannot live without you. You told me that you would be unable to come without any women that you know!! But of course you know well that there are enough women here as to help you. Do you think that the "middle east" is full of males only??*

*I don't know exactly what I am going to do after I finish the exams, but I think it would be better if you tell me in your next letter of the time of your coming.*

*How is your girl friend Faye? I hope that she had at last discovered the one who truly loves her. But you are certainly aware that a girl can feel and know quite well the true lover. Don't you agree with me??*

*My love, Be cautious as far as her two brothers. I felt jealous when I read that you went to have a game of tennis with them. Stick to tennis only!!!!*

*I want to end my letter, but in fact I want to write again and again. The words, my darling, will fail to express what is really within my heart.*

*I will be in Jordan on the 20th of June. Of course you know my address there, Hanna Farraj, Jericho, Jordan. I think it is too short if you want to send any cable.*

*My best wishes to your family, and my warmest kisses to you, and I remain*

*Yours forever,*
*Hanna*
*XXXXXX*
*XXXX*
*XX*
*X*

*May 21st, 1960*

*My dearest love,*

*Hanna darling, I want to write to you because I want you to always remember that I love you and am thinking of the promise we hold, however words seem so silly and meaningless. I would so much rather be near you and stay there forever and ever!*

*Hanna, do you know any more? Could you come all right if I'd send you the money? Or shall I make definite plans to come to you? As I believe I've said before, it would save us so much money if you came. Otherwise it would be 3 trips to pay. And I have to ask my father and I am almost sure he will do it, but he is not happy about it.*

*However it is, it must be!! Sometimes I feel like calling you a (SHATON) That's an Arabic word. Do you recognize it? (I hope it's the right word, I'm forgetting Arabic fast.) Because I remember how determined I was not to fall in love with you! Because I just did not think it would work. But some how you convinced me that you are the most wonderful man I know!! And now I'm mad about you. You get in my thoughts continually and I can't ever think things out straight anymore. I'm glad I don't have to study for exams. But I hope that they went well for you. I do hope you succeeded.*

*Please write back immediately and tell me these answers if you haven't already. Can you really get a visa if I would send money to you? Or if I come to you? And if so how long would I stay? etc? Because it's time to make definite plans and I'm so excited.*

*I'm worried about the world and all its problems. So I don't think we should waste time getting together because who knows what will happen?*

*With my thoughts and devotion and love,*
*Myrna XXX*

(On the outside flaps of the Air Letter:)

*I would write here also but I'm afraid someone will read this. If I only had a picture of you smiling. I look at all the pictures I have of you and I tell them to please smile at me but they refuse. I talk to your picture all the time. (Now you know how silly I am!) I say, Hanna Darling, please be happy because "I love you to the height and depth and breadth my soul can reach" "I love thee with the breath, smiles, tears, of all my life!" I love thee.*

*I had a letter and picture from Hannieh Kawas. She is a dear friend of mine. She said that she and Sophie are not coming to the states after all. I am mad at Mr. Lehman about it. Next weekend I may see the Lehmans. They are in Indiana right now. And I want to go to a girl friend's wedding. I hope they ask me about you and me so I can tell them that I plan to marry Hanna just as I wanted to in Jordan. (only much more now do I want to.) XXX*

*Cairo*
*3rd of June, 1960*

*My dearest love,*

    *I received your letter dated 21st of May 1960. I am sorry not answering your letter immediately, but you know that I am going to sit for the examinations after one week.*

    *You told me in your letter to answer all the questions you want and I think I answered all the questions in my last letter, which you are going to receive after your last letter to me.*

    *Here I want to say again that I failed to get any kind of Visa to USA and I think there isn't any other salve, only you have to come to me immediately. I told you that I am going to be in Jordan after three weeks, so you have to answer my letter very soon to receive your answer before I leave, to know what to do and to prepare for everything.*

    *My friend George is still in Cairo and he is going to leave it with me, and he send to you his best wishes. I don't know what you are doing now. Are you still working? Or what? Where do you spend most of your time? I have nothing to say, just I want you to be near me very soon——then I can do what I want and say all the twenty-five love words to you.*

    *My best wishes to your father and mother wishing them the good health and the strong desire for life.*

    *My love to your sister and all your friends.*

*From your mad Arabian Lover*
*Hanna*
*XXXXX*
*XXX*
*X*

    *P.S. I saw a lovely film last night, the name of this film is "BELOVED INFIDEL." Have you seen it?*

*June 5th, 1960*

*My dearest Hanna,*

*I'm writing you two identical letters, one I'm sending to Jordan and one to Egypt, because I was not quite sure where you are. You wrote you would be in Jordan the 26th of June but I thought perhaps you meant May because you wrote I could send a telegram to Jordan. So just in case I'd send to the wrong place I'll write two letters.*

*I don't know what to say because nothing is definite as yet, but I want to write so you know I'm trying. My father told me I must find out in more details if there will be a waiting period after I enter the Middle East before we can marry and if it is certain that I can return immediately and then file the papers. He said he wouldn't give the money for a ticket until we are more certain.*

*I didn't know how to find out, but there is a very nice lady working where I do whose husband is a professor in the University. I told her about us, and what I want to know, so she is asking law-yer friends that teach law at the University. Tomorrow I should know what help they can give.*

*So I talked to the travel agent and he told me jets leave Chicago on Mondays at 8:00P.M. and arrive in Beirut at 6:00 Tuesdays but it is all filled through June and the first part of July. So all I can do is put my name on the waiting list and hope someone places a cancellation.*

*If things would work out (Inshallah!!) I will leave Chicago the evening of July 4th and arrive in Beirut the evening of July 5th (one month from today!) Will you meet me? Perhaps you know something about this waiting time to get married, etc. My father is afraid I'll have to stay 6 months. I'm so afraid something will happen. I can only pray. I only have 2 weeks from work or I will lose my job. I will send you a telegram later to tell you if things can work out.*

*Write Darling. I love you SO much,*
*Myrna*


*P.S. It may have to be later in July if there is no place on the plane but I hope not.*


(on flap:)
*Monday Morning:*
*I opened this to add that Dear Mrs. Major talked to the man about us. He assured her that there would be no trouble once we are married, but he wondered if it might be possible to get married by proxy. Which would mean I'd fill papers here and you would there and they would be authorized and recognized as a marriage. He suggested that each consulate in every country is different but it might be worth looking in to. So if you'd like to see. But I'll go ahead with the plans. They thought maybe I didn't want to go that far in case you might stand me up and not be there. But I think I could take a chance on that.*
*Also, he wondered of the possibility of you getting a visa to Mexico. See you very soon,*

*Love, Myrna*
*(Identical letter to Egypt)*

*June 17th, 1960*

*My dearest love,*

*Yesterday morning I arrived Jerusalem from Cairo. I received both of your two letters, the first in Cairo and the other in Jericho. I was really happy when you told me that you are going to come in July, but in the same time you asked me if we could get married by Proxy. Tell now, I know nothing about this, but after a few days I want to go to Amman to ask about it, and about all the questions you want to know.*

*Last night we talked about our marriage. All my family agreed and they promised me to make me happy when you will be in Jordan.*

*I have nothing to do now, just waiting your arrival, and I am going to come with my sister to Beirut to meet you. I am coming in our new car. It is a Volkswagen 1960. I don't know what to say to you, but I am still dreaming about that lovely moment when we will be together holding——kissing each other. I like kissing very much! Don't you? You didn't tell me about your work, what kinds of work? Is it easy work? I hope that you are happy in your life now.*

*At the end I wish your parents the good health and a happy life. My best wishes to your sweet sister and her husband.*

*Don't be late. I adore you!!*
*From your mad Arabian Lover,*
*Hanna*

*P.S. Darling, Hanna Ammar came to my house last night. He tried to convince me that he is a good friend to me. He asked me to tell you that he is sorry about all his wrong deeds towards you and me. But I told him that I am inviting him to our marriage in July. Don't you think that it is good of me to invite him!!!*
*Yours forever*

# 25

# RETURN TO JERICHO

MY DECISION WAS made. I'd stand by my word. I had written Hanna that if no other method would work for us to get together, I'd go to him in the summer. We had thought of many options but none proved feasible. Going to him in Jericho was what I'd do.

The job I had taken at the University Testing Service after returning to Iowa didn't provide me with enough money to pay for my trip. Always my preference was to be as independent as possible, but I saw no choice. I'd need to seek my parents' financial help. Along with the needed money I hoped to gain their approval.

It wasn't easy for me to approach them and discuss my decision. My parents had heard about John from the time Hannieh, Sophie, and I made our afternoon visit to the Farraj home in Jericho. Back in June of 1959, when I first agreed to marry him, I wrote them the details. It was evident that the news had upset my mother enough to cause her to destroy the letter with the information.

Not long after I sent that disturbing letter, I wrote them again stating that my promise to Hanna no longer held. It was apparent they were relieved when Mr. Lehman stepped in and put a stop to what they must've thought was an irrational decision on my part.

After I returned to Iowa they knew John and I were writing, but I didn't share with them my growing passion for him. I was still too unsure about what direction the relationship was going. Not long after Hanna wrote my father a letter vowing his love for me, my parents and I had a long talk.

"I need to go back to Jericho to marry Hanna. There's no other way. We thought of many plans to get together, but none will work. I must go to him, and I'll need your help."

My mother's reaction was expected. "Are you quite sure you want to marry him? You want to marry someone from another country? Someone we know nothing about?"

"Yes, Mom, I'm sure."

"But think what people will say. It will be the talk of the community. I can just hear your Grandmother Kinsinger and Aunt Orpha's opinions."

"People can say whatever they want to say. My grandma and Aunt Orpha will be fine with it. No one can discourage me. I will marry John Farraj."

I knew my father understood my feelings, that I loved Hanna and wanted to marry him. But his mind was full of questions. "If you're determined to do this, how will your plan work out? Can you go there and come right back, or will you have to stay a length of time following the wedding? You need to remember you signed a contract to teach. You have to be sure that you get yourself back in time."

"I'm not sure if there's a time limit, but I'll find out the details."

"You'll have to go alone. It'll be a sacrifice for us to find the money for your plane flight. Can't he come here to marry you? That would be a sensible solution."

Knowing my father well, I anticipated this reaction. He would want details. To him it would seem impractical and expensive for me to return to Jericho. I could tell my dad was thinking, *If the guy is really serious about marrying my daughter, and if he plans to live here, he'll find a way to come. Why does she need to go back? Why spend money for three flights across the Atlantic when only one is needed?* My father was a generous man but also very practical.

I felt encouraged because I knew he was compassionate by nature. Always, he'd treated me with affection, as his special little girl—his right hand. Growing up, I'd spent more time with him than anyone else. He had no sons, so I was more than happy to fill that void on the farm, working with him every chance I got.

I had many precious memories being with him, tagging along to hand him the tools when he made fences, whacking off thistles with him in the sweltering pasture after a rainy night, driving the Model A Ford out into the fields to give the workers water even though I barely reached the clutch. Being with my daddy is where I loved to be more than anywhere else. Now I needed to depend on him and my mother to fulfill the commitment I'd made to Hanna.

It had to be scary for my parents to think their daughter would take this leap of faith. They knew nothing about John except what I told them, and they assumed my opinions were biased. They likely were going through doubts about his sincerity. I'd worked through those doubts with months of prayer. *God, it's in your hands. May your will be done.* I had all confidence that I was taking the right step.

Unknown to me, they'd sought advice. After seeking council with our pastor, my parents seemed at peace, were supportive of my decision, and gave me the means to make the trip to Jericho.

With fast action I pulled a wardrobe together, not really knowing what would be appropriate. I hoped I was covering my needs for all the possible upcoming occasions. Hanna's family and circle of friends would be more dressed-up in the latest fashions than was my usual style. There was no way around it—I'd need to take heels, even if they hurt my feet.

I visited our family doctor, who was also the president of the school board that had just hired me for the coming year. Dr. Miller chatted as he fitted me with a diaphragm, more or less the only birth control of the day. At that time the school didn't like to hire married teachers, and definitely a pregnant teacher was unacceptable.

Since he knew my family well and had been my biggest recommendation for the job, he was accepting my marriage, although I could sense his doubts about its wisdom. I heard the message he was sending me. *Will you be able to handle being a wife and a teacher both? And what will you do if you get pregnant? How do you think the school will accept that?* I listened politely, but nothing could dissuade me from heading off to marry the man I was certain I wanted for my lifetime partner.

On July 6th, 1960, I left Cedar Rapids by plane to Chicago. Instead of a simple change of gates in The Windy City, I had to catch a taxi from the Midway airport to O'Hare for the second leg to New York City. There, I had to get on a bus to change terminals for the Pan Am flight to Beirut, Lebanon. I'd then board a small aircraft from Beirut into Jerusalem. This was my first time traveling by air, and it included not one but four different planes. Managing this trip would be no small matter. But I was willing to brave anything to reach the love of my life.

After what seemed like a long, tedious journey I arrived in Beirut. There I was met with the unexplained news that the plane to Jerusalem was delayed until the following day. *Oh no! Horrors! This can't be! I want to get there. This is sad!*

Upon this information the doubts began to creep in. I spent a restless night at an airport hotel with my nerves on edge. *Am I doing the right thing? Does his family really want me to come?*

On the plane into Jerusalem the next day, I continued to be anxious about how things would go. *Has his family accepted for him to marry me? Am I too bold to travel here alone? Will they think so? How will they treat me? Am I going to know how to handle everything?* And then the worst scare yet came as we were circling for a landing. *What if I don't recognize which one is Hanna? It was a year ago when I saw him, and then for only a month.*

The plane landed in Jerusalem. As I descended the steps from the aircraft, I scanned the grounds with nervous tension. There he was! The first one I spotted! No more doubts! He'd somehow gained permission to meet me as I exited the plane. I couldn't keep my eyes off him. All my anxieties were gone.

He looked even better than I remembered. With a big, reassuring smile illuminating his face he greeted me, *"Ahlan wa sahlan!* Welcome, *Habibti!"*

In his usual take-charge mode, Hanna assisted me through customs and out to meet his family, who'd come to the airport to greet me. His sister Samira and his mother and father welcomed me with gracious respect. I met his brother Samir, who seemed fantastic—and was handsome, too. But no one looked as good as the man I'd come to marry. We were on our way to Jericho. *God is good! This is where I belong.*

Before I left the States, I'd signed a contract to teach fourth grade in Williamsburg, Iowa, starting around the middle of August. Because of this I'd given myself only two weeks in Jordan. This meant we had to move fast with the wedding plans.

It was the local custom to spend the week before the wedding celebrating, but in this case first came the preparations. To complicate matters, this was July in Jericho, most likely the hottest spot on earth. No one seemed to notice the heat, although the roof ended up to be the place where people preferred to sleep when night came.

There were many details to accomplish in the nine days between when I arrived and the day we set for the wedding. I was oblivious to most of the plans. In part it was because my Arabic wasn't good enough to follow their fast conversations.

My thoughts: *I don't need to slow them down to ask every trivial question about the plans. Their son will soon be leaving them and coming to live with me in the States. They know the customs for a wedding. I don't. They deserve the privilege of planning the occasion they will want to remember.* You could say I was along for the ride. And what a grand ride it was!

Back in the winter months when I was mulling my decision about taking this big step, I'd been helped by the thought that if Hanna turns out like his father I wasn't making a mistake. Elias Farraj,

Hanna's father, was a man I held in high esteem. Abu Samir, as he was known, was a gentle, compassionate, thoughtful person. He showed me those traits as we rushed to make the wedding plans.

*Hanna's Father, Elias Farraj*

Abu Samir knew I was Protestant and had taught in the Anglican school in Amman. He took us to St. George's Compound in Jerusalem to see if there we could marry. I knew the place well as it was a spot I'd visited many times. To have our wedding at St. George's would be comfortable and delightful for me. However, we found it couldn't happen there, as the Church of England required banns read two weeks prior to the wedding as a public announcement. This gave an opportunity for anyone's objections to the marriage to be stated. That meant the beautiful cathedral was out of the question, as we didn't have the necessary two-week time span period to read the banns.

Abu Samir, in his thoughtful way, turned to me inquiring, "Since it doesn't work out in the Protestant church, Myrna, will you accept to have the wedding in our Jericho Greek Orthodox Church?"

"Yes, I'm more than willing!" was my ready reply. "I came a long way to marry your son whom I love. To me it makes no difference where it happens."

That same day, while in Jerusalem, we went into the Old City to buy the supplies for making the traditional mementos: candy-covered almonds, chocolates, small plates, and the cellophane paper with ribbon to tie it all together. These small plates of sweets would then be given out at the wedding to show the guests that their attendance was valued.

As plans developed, it became obvious the small Jericho Greek Orthodox Church wouldn't hold the people that wished to attend this unique wedding. Family and friends wanted to see their favorite Jericho boy—the lad that stirred up the world with his causes—marry the American girl, who they knew all about as she'd worked with the Mennonites and their endeavors. So the plans were quickly altered to the Hisham White Palace Hotel.

A special request was made for the Jerusalem Greek Orthodox patriarch to be in charge of the marriage, with the assistance of the local colorful Greek priest. Over three hundred invitations were ordered, some in Arabic and others in English:

John E. Farraj
and
Myrna Kinsinger
request the honour of your presence
at their wedding ceremony
on Sunday the 17th of July, 1960
at 5:00 p.m.
at the White Palace Hotel, Jericho

# 26

# A FLURRY OF ACTIVITIES

JUST MINUTES FROM Jericho lies the lowest spot on earth, the Dead Sea. The first night I arrived, we went with friends swimming in the salty sea with a full moon overhead and background music floating from the nearby hotels. Oh, how I loved Hanna's delicious saline kisses. No more doubts! No more anxieties! I was where I wanted to be.

A few days later, Abu Samir took us to the gold shop in Amman to get rings. Our simple, identical gold bands had our initials etched inside each other's ring, with the wedding date done in the European style, 17/7/60. Upon getting our new rings, we slipped them on each other's right hands, right in the middle of the *souk*.

Tradition was that the ring was worn on the right hand as a sign of engagement and moved to the left hand upon marriage. We knew our rings wouldn't be staying long on our right hands. This was a small detail, but it left me giddy with happiness.

*Rings on our Right Hands*

While in Amman they rented for me a wedding dress. I'd taken a short, white batiste cotton frock that could be used for any occasion. Having had no idea how things would go, I was thinking of the wedding as some simple, quiet ceremony, perhaps for just the family. Little did I know that five hundred people would witness my becoming Mrs. John Farraj. I was quite happy with the dress, as it was pretty and fit me fine, although I didn't completely fill out the bodice. The dress made me smile. It may be the only time in my life I was a double D.

That evening, Jericho family friends came over to help prepare the traditional sweets for the wedding. Many hands joined in the task of arranging the sugarcoated almonds around a chocolate on a small, painted china plate. It was then covered with cellophane and tied with a ribbon. One would be given out to each guest as a wedding memento. It was an evening of preparation that turned into an evening of celebration. Soon the drum was sounding, and singing and dancing followed, with the local friends joining in.

The uncles and aunts descended on Jericho to see me for the first time. The Farraj clan is large and close-knit. In the customary Arab traditional thinking, they'd planned from Hanna's birth the cousin he should marry. Now there were more than a few doubts about this turn of events; it wasn't part of what they saw as the foreseeable future for their darling nephew, Hanna Farraj.

I got giggly as I could tell they were looking me up and down to see if they approved or not. There was little doubt but that Hanna was their favorite. With his usual charm he made each feel special. He was known as a daringly honest person with strong opinions, quick to speak and wise beyond his years. I could see them thinking, *How can this American girl come and take our pet away from us?*

I'm glad I couldn't understand the true gist of what they were saying as they took their time with their scrutinizing inspections. Yes, they saw that my legs were not one of my best features, a little on the heavy side. But I knew that already. *Where else am I lacking in reaching your standards? Let's admit it, I'll never live up to your expectations.*

It seemed I passed the test; they accepted me. I was thankful, of course. However, for me there was only one test important to pass. I had full confidence that with Hanna I scored high off the chart.

Flowers were ordered and dresses were sewn. Aunt Aujeneh from Amman was solicited to help with the selection of material. Before she married Abu Samir's youngest brother, she'd been the seamstress for many high-society families, including some of the royal family. She was the magician at the sewing machine and created the bridesmaid dress for Samira, which was later to be my going-away dress.

It was our good fortune that Samira and I were the same size, but Aunty measured and fit the dress on both of us. In short order she created a street-length dress of light-green damascene silk brocade with a removable peplum. She also designed a cummerbund and a bow for the back so it could be worn in different ways.

By this time, many people had congregated in Jericho. The Farraj clan is large. Folks came from Madaba, Irbid, Mafrak, Salt, and Amman. For them it was celebration time, and they were ready to party.

With the many people gathering, the women were preparing food without end. Everyone helped out, and things fell into place like magic. The ladies made the special Arabic dishes: stuffed grape leaves, *kibbie*, rice and lamb, hummus, baba ghanouj. Amazing amounts of people were around who needed breakfast, lunch, and dinner. And, of course, Arabic coffee was served at all hours. With help from many hands, there was always more than enough food to satisfy everyone.

Neither Hanna nor I had an appetite for food. I could've lived solely on being next to Hanna with my eyes on him. Standards dictated that we needed to keep our affection in control while with the family and friends. This was complicated by there being no place to be alone. There were people everywhere. So we followed what was expected of us, which only stirred our desire for each other a notch higher.

Another prewedding evening was spent at Hanna's friend Tony's father's farm just outside Jericho. This was a large fruit farm with three houses, a swimming pool, and entertainment area. The United Nations diplomatic workers that kept security in the region occupied one of the houses. The event of notability that evening was when one of the tall, Australian UN workers challenged John's oldest uncle, Abu Galeb, to arm wrestling. A case of Scotch was the wager set. Much to the surprise of the big, burly Ausie, Abu Galeb took him down with a snap. This turned into a famed story that's related to this day.

Evening after evening found the family and friends at the Farraj residence in celebration mode. Music was everywhere, with people playing the *oud* (lute) and the *tablah* (drum). Many voices accompanied the spontaneous dancing. Women and girls did the belly dance; young men joined in to serenade them. All banded together in the *debke,* the line dance that is traditional at weddings. By insistence of the gathering, one evening I did a short attempt at the belly dance. You would've thought I did fine by the cheers and applause that came my way.

Evenings ended with everyone sleeping on the roof with extra mattresses supplied by the small hotel next door. The hotel was also fully occupied by the rest of the large Farraj clan.

Because it was very hot in Jericho, the refrigerator was well stocked with bottles filled with water. I had become fascinated by their custom of drinking from the bottles. The method was to throw your head back, open your mouth wide, hold the bottle high above you, and let the water flow down into your mouth without your lips touching the bottle.

No one was in the kitchen. It was my chance to attempt this unique method of drinking. However it wasn't water in the bottle I grabbed, but *Arak,* a strong, clear, colorless, unsweetened anise-flavored aperitif that's 126 proof. When the liquid hit my throat it felt like fire. I let out a bloody scream!

Hanna's mother came running to save me. She couldn't hold back her laughter as she attempted to soothe me and explain the mystery of the mixed up identical bottles.

It became an amusing story that got told and retold. Probably you could say it was my induction into the Farraj family. In spite of my embarrassment, from that moment on I felt completely adored and accepted by everyone.

*With Hanna's Mother, Shafika Farraj*

By the morning of the wedding we realized more people were coming than previously thought and there wouldn't be enough mementos. Since no one knew the shops like Hanna, he was the one who needed to go back to Jerusalem to buy additional supplies.

This day was busy for him, as tradition had it that on the groom's wedding day he was given his last bath as a single man by the men in the family. I'm not sure what all took place, but I know the young cousins had a lot of fun with that part of the morning.

He was exhausted from running to Jerusalem and accomplishing numerous last-minute tasks. To top it all off, in his excitement he'd cut himself rather badly shaving. All this was while I did nothing but whatever someone led me to do. They took me to the beauty parlor and attempted to get me looking as good as possible.

That morning, Hanna's brother, his father, and an uncle privately asked me to come with them out on the balcony. Dr. Samir began, "Myrna, we want you to know that just because you are here and all the plans are made doesn't mean you have to go through with the wedding. We know John is young and has done some impulsive things in his short life. You can still change your mind if you wish."

*Wow!* That was hard for me to comprehend. *Are they saying they don't want him to marry me? No way will I back out. I came all this way to marry the man I love. And I will marry him! Nothing will change my mind.* Without hesitation that's what I told them.

Later John explained that in his high school days he'd been involved with the revolutionists and their political causes. As a young man of means he was ready to fight for more rights for the Palestinian refugees living in the nearby camps.

We were going to America for the time being, but I was willing to come back to live in Jordan in a heartbeat. I related to the Palestinian cause and was more than willing to spend my life for it if that's what John wanted us to do at some juncture in our lives.

He convinced me that his family wasn't against our marriage but that they wanted me to understand about his past involvements. They had to be sad he would be leaving, and I felt sad for them. They needed to be assured I was serious about marrying their son the same as my parents had wanted to know John's intentions and sincerity. It felt good that I had a chance to let them know I was committed to our future together, and that I trusted he would be my companion for life.

# 27

# FROM MISS TO MRS.

THE BIG MOMENT had arrived. It was our wedding day. Very soon I'd be a married woman. No longer would I be Miss Myrna Marie Kinsinger.

First came the big feast with not one but three lambs butchered and turned into three *mansufs* for the large gathering. *Mansuf* is the traditional Bedouin meal served for royalty and for all special celebrations. It's a mounded bed of rice on flat bread with the lamb piled on top. Hot yogurt is then poured over the dish. To top it all off, it's covered with roasted pine nuts. This meal is traditionally eaten with the hand by forming a small, round ball of the ingredients.

I was much too excited to eat, but I couldn't escape the small balls of *mansuf* prepared for me by members of the family. By popping a ball of *mansuf* into my mouth with their hand, they were displaying their love and acceptance of me and of our marriage. No way could I refuse bite after bite offered me. It was a blessing that Hanna kept a lookout and saved me when I was struggling from being overfed. With all the family and friends present, the three large trays of *mansuf* were easily devoured.

And then there were gifts. Hanna's mother and father came, planting kisses on my cheeks and placing six gold bangles on my wrist. His mother's parents, along with the unmarried uncle and aunt, George and Georgette, presented me with a tray of rings, maybe at least a dozen. "Pick out the one you want, Myrna. This is our present for you."

I was overwhelmed! I'd never seen such an array of gorgeous, large rings before in my life. Being put on the spot, and not being one for extravagance, I went for the smallest one I could see. As it turned out, it's an Alexandrite stone set in 24-karat gold, which no one has ever called small to this day. Its characteristic is that it changes color from a light hue in the sunlight to a purplish red in incandescent light.

The aunts and uncles came to give me presents. From the uncles I received gold bracelets, which were almost too beautiful to wear. There were a few other presents but mostly the gifts were cash. All were more than appreciated for their love and good wishes.

After the feast, it was time to get dressed and head for the wedding. We women were in the lead car that led a long parade to the hotel, where the altar was set up for the Orthodox ceremony. It was a big hall but still not spacious enough for all the people plus chairs. So the simple solution—no chairs. The guests, as well as the wedding party, remained standing throughout the ceremony.

Dr. Samir Farraj, Hanna's only brother, was his best man. Samira, Hanna's only sister, was my maid of honor. The Greek Orthodox patriarch of Jerusalem took his job seriously, and the ceremony lasted at least an hour. All this happened in the late-afternoon July heat of over 100 degrees Fahrenheit with no air conditioning. No one left. No one fainted. Everyone endured to the end.

*Arriving at the White Palace Hotel with Hanna's Siblings*

My memories of our wedding ceremony are scattered and hazy, rather like being in a dream. What do I remember? Foremost, I remember the perspiration flowing down my front between my breasts. As hot as I was, I couldn't imagine how Hanna and his brother were feeling in their three-piece suits.

I remember the patriarch placing crowns on our heads with a ribbon connecting them. Then we, with our attendants, followed him around the altar three times, all in the name of God the Father, the Son, and the Holy Spirit. The patriarch served us communion by placing the wafers in our mouths and tipping the cup up to our lips.

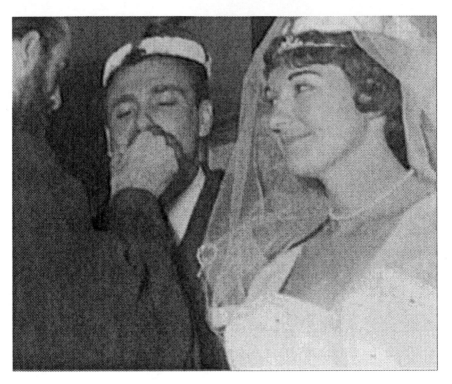

*Receiving Communion from the Patriarch*

I understood nothing being said, as most of it was in Greek and the rest in classical Arabic. There were no questions inquired of us, and we never were asked to respond. I remember peeking at Hanna and thinking, *He looks so tired!* I remember being ecstatically happy, feeling content and secure with Hanna by my side, but a little confused. *I don't understand anything. Are we married yet? How will I know when it happens?*

Sometime during the ceremony an aunt basted my dress to Hanna's suit jacket at the hipline in the rite of sewing us together for life. I was relieved when the ceremony was over and we walked outside and stood in a receiving line for guests to come shake our hands and give us their best wishes. The large extended family and close friends who'd been part of the prewedding celebrations and had eaten the *mansuf* with us had earlier bestowed their well wishes. So here it was the guests, both Christian and Muslim, other than family and those close to us, who wanted to wish us a happy marriage.

*Our Receiving Line after the Ceremony*

We signed our names on the marriage papers. The documents, also signed by the patriarch and our witnesses, made it all official in the eyes of God, the church, the country of Jordan, and the US consulate.

Following the ceremony, the MCC unit members held for us an American-style reception in the Jericho MCC house. Early on they'd asked us to make up a guest list of close family and friends that we'd like to have with us at this small reception. They knew traditional Arab celebrations had gone on before the wedding; in fact they'd attended some of them. But they wanted to be my connection to home since I had no family with me.

The reception was lovely, with a dazzling cake, nuts, mints, juice, and coffee. The Lehmans were on leave back in the States, so it was twins Ida and Ada who oversaw this delightful event that touched my heart. Hannieh and Sophie and all my special friends were there to cheer me on. They were my family and looked after my needs. Here we got some of our best photographs for memories. This reception provided a time for Hanna and me to unwind, relax, and begin enjoying each other.

*Relaxing at the MCC Reception*

What had happened in the last nine days had been like a sweltering tsunami coming through. We'd survived! I was the lucky one, hardly lifting a hand to do anything. It was John who'd made sure everything was planned and went off successfully. He was exhausted but covered it up well. It seemed unbelievable that our marriage had actually happened, that the dream that began a little over a year before had now come true.

After Hanna found the car keys, which in his excitement he'd misplaced for the umpteenth time, we were on our way out of Jericho, through Jerusalem, to Ramallah for our honeymoon. Ramallah, an hour away in the mountains, is much cooler than Jericho. But best of all, at last we could be alone.

A friend had made reservations for us at the Grand Hotel for dinner and dancing. We spent a minimal time there, then on to the beautiful Harb Hotel for our first night to discover our joy of wedded love. We'd overcome many obstacles. The struggle had been long and difficult, but it was fulfilled at last. *Thank You, God!*

It was back to Jerusalem the following morning to savor a delectable breakfast of hummus with lamb kidneys and Rocky Mountain oysters, Hanna's favorite. We needed to be in Jerusalem to register our marriage at the US consulate. That proved a simple formality necessary for the papers I'd be preparing when I returned to Iowa. After the papers were accepted, John could get a visa and enter the United States as my husband.

In only a few more days I'd need to leave Jordan and return to Iowa. We spent the last days relaxing with his close family. Hanna's mother and father had to be more than exhausted from the intense time handling all the arrangements and activities in such a short span of time.

It was my joy that John would be coming to live with me in Iowa. Even though his parents never showed me unhappiness about our future plans, I felt a deep sadness for them. They would miss their youngest child. He was a dynamic force of love and action in their lives.

I'd have liked for him to be traveling back with me, but it was good he needed to stay longer. This could soften the blow for his family and give them a little more time together. With him they'd be celebrating his twenty-first birthday on September 15, most likely their last chance at giving him a birthday party.

The night before my departure, aunts and uncles returned to Jericho to bid me farewell. Once more, Hanna's mother and sister prepared a lavish meal for the occasion, and the evening turned into more singing and dancing. And once more the roof was the destination for sleep for most everyone except Hanna and me. We preferred our privacy, no matter how hot the room.

The day for me to leave was an emotional one. I felt content and happy and sad all at the same time. The family's graciousness in accepting me and making me feel their comfort and love was beyond measure.

Once more, the extended family surrounded us at the Jerusalem airport to wait out my time of departure. It was sad for me to say good-bye to the family and leave John behind and board the plane. I wasn't looking forward to reversing my trip back to Beirut, across the Atlantic to New York to change terminals, on to Chicago to change airports, and then the last leg to Cedar Rapids. I'd be arriving home to find my parents, my sister, and her family eagerly waiting to hear every detail of my adventure.

Upon returning to Iowa I worked as quickly as possible to fill out the proper papers to bring my husband, John E. Farraj, to the States. Meanwhile I began my new job of preparing a classroom, meeting my twenty-eight fourth graders, and settling into teaching. That needed my full attention.

I filed the necessary papers and sent them off to the proper site. John received his visa and arrived at the Cedar Rapids airport on October 1, 1960. The blissful joy I felt at being united with my love was sublime.

It was no surprise to me that my parents and sister's family all loved John from the moment he arrived. Without any difficulty he won them over to being his enthusiastic fans.

Within a week my parents had a reception for us with the eager extended family and friends coming to meet and learn to know Myrna's exotic husband. Now it was John's turn to pass inspection, which he did with great ease. An added benefit was that the reception supplied us with the basic gifts we'd need to start our household.

The first year was a busy one. We moved from living with my parents on the farm to an apartment in Williamsburg where I was teaching. John enrolled in the University of Iowa for the second semester. Soon we discovered that, in spite of protection, I was pregnant. Together we set out on our life's journey. *Praise God! We are blessed!*

# 28

## THE AFTERWORD

On Love

Love gives naught but itself
And takes naught but from itself.
Love possesses not nor would it be possessed,
For love is sufficient unto love.
When you love you should not say, "God is in my heart,"
But rather, "I am in the heart of God."
And think not you can direct the course of love,
For love, if it finds you worthy, directs your course.

—Kahlil Gibran from *The Prophet*

IT'S NOW LATER than my story by fifty-plus years. I won't profess the journey between our wedding day and the present as sunny and wonderful. It's been raw life, with its struggles, disappointments, blessings, beauty, sorrow, and joy. My love for John has grown in a different dimension and surpasses the love of that day long ago. Through it all, I thank God again and again for leading me to Hanna, to the love he's shown me, and to the lessons I've learned as his wife and by being the mother of his children. I wouldn't want to be anywhere but where this love has taken me.

What I'd gleaned about John from the short time we spent together and from our letters told me everything I needed to know. I love his strength of character, his confidence, and his ambition and determination. He's someone who makes up his mind quickly, gives an opinion, and sticks with it. He's a type-A personality, a driver, a perfectionist, and an impatient person with a short temper.

These traits served him well. There were many barriers he faced in coming to America: no close family here, an incomplete college education, a need to master English, early responsibilities of a family, no viable connections, and a lack of knowledge about the way things work in America. In spite of all obstacles, he's been highly successful in the life insurance and financial planning industry where his charisma and sharp mind combined to provide a good life for our family.

Family has been of prime importance to him. He has steadfast loyalty to his upbringing and those that were part of his being. He placed that same loyalty in the family we created. Charles John, known as Chuck, was born a year after our marriage. Three years later, we were blessed with Anthony John, called Tony, and five years after that along came Rima Jane. All were wonderful additions to our lives and taught us many lessons.

We are honored to have three granddaughters, Jordan, Mia, and Eva, and three grandsons, Christian, Anders, and Hans. We pray that the inspiration of our lives and the strength of our legacy will live on through them.

We had many differences. He was a city boy. I was a farm girl. He came from the privileged class of his society; I from the humble working class. He was an extrovert, outgoing and charismatic. I was an introvert, shy and at times inhibited. He had ready responses. I could become tongue-tied. He knew how he felt on every issue. I saw two sides of most anything. We'd been raised in differing cultural and religious traditions, although the same in basic beliefs. These were amazing contrasts in our lives. Yet our differences never stood in our way, but rather we adapted and learned from each other.

At times his perfectionism and impatience have been hard for me. I sensed he wanted me to be a perfect wife. There were numerous times I didn't live up to what he thought that meant, and I felt his disappointment. I had within me that independent and creative spirit that inwardly rebelled against someone expecting me to be a certain way. At the same time, I hated conflict and could be intimidated to withdraw from disagreements. Nevertheless, through the trials that came I never doubted his love for me or my love for him.

I'm grateful to have had my work as an educator. My career saved my sanity by giving me an outlet for my individuality and creativity. Yet with the concentration I put in my job, I lived with the ever-present concern that I was giving too little time and energy to our children. In spite of our shortcomings, they developed into beautiful human beings. Through it all, my strong faith in God and my belief in the divine leading of my life gave me peace and kept me strong, confident, content, and full of joy.

The Six-Day War of 1967, followed by the Israeli military occupation of the West Bank, changed our world. John's mother and father were in Amman for medical appointments at the onset of the conflict and never returned to their Jericho home, but remained living in Amman with their son, John's brother, Dr. Samir Farraj. In the early years, we didn't have money to return often to the Middle East. Even telephone conversations required quick talking and were typically reserved for holidays. In later years, we were able to visit Amman more often and also returned back through Jericho to the much loved holy spots. We treasure the times when our Farraj family visit us in Iowa. We have a deep sadness and a prayer for peace in the land.

John and I are bound together by common beliefs. We look to the importance of faith, compassion, loyalty, justice, trust, family, and a positive hope for the future. Both of us are ready for adventure, challenges, and new horizons. Always our salvation has been that we encourage each other to live our own lives, to go our own ways, and to be our own persons. Then we come back to each other renewed.

## On Marriage

But let there be spaces in your togetherness,
And let the winds of the heavens dance between you.
Love one another, but make not a bond of love:
Let it rather be a moving sea between the shores of your souls.
Fill each other's cup but drink not from one cup.
Give one another of your bread but eat not from the same loaf.
Sing and dance together and be joyous,
But let each one of you be alone.
Even as the strings of a lute are alone
Though they quiver with the same music.
Give your hearts, but not into each other's keeping.
For only the hand of Life can contain your hearts.
And stand together, yet not too near together:
For the pillars of the temple stand apart,
And the oak tree and the cypress grow not in each other's shadow.

—Kahlil Gibran from *The Prophet*

*50th Wedding Anniversary, Summer 2010*

# ACKNOWLEDGMENTS

My story is possible because of my experiences with the Mennonite Central Committee and their commitment to peace and world relief. I'm thankful for being accepted into the group for the two years I spent with them. I respect their work and am humbly proud to have served with the MCC.

As this was in an era long before e-mails, and even telephoning was out of the question, I was obligated to write weekly letters to my family. I'm thankful to my grandparents, my aunts, my sister, and my parents for saving the letters—well, almost all of them. It's from these letters that my memories came. It's a blessing that they expected me to write and relate details about my adventures.

That I kept every letter from Hanna is quite expected, but that he kept every letter of mine I found endearing. John arrived in the States with only one suitcase, and the fact that a string-tied bundle of my letters was in it made my heart happy. We think we have most of the correspondence that reached us during the year we wrote, although there were telegrams we didn't save. The letters are unedited. They appear exactly as we wrote them. It was tempting to change some lines (such as "Europe is a beautiful country"), but I refrained.

Over the years our friends and acquaintances knew very little of the details of our story. My friend Marilyn Wirtz learned a little more than most. I wouldn't have written these memoirs without her urging and belief that I could and should do it. Jan Down, another friend, encouraged me to join the University Club Writers' Group when I shared with her that I wanted to work on my memoirs. It was with them that I first began having fun writing and sharing. The women of the club were patient and encouraging, while at the same time correcting and teaching me. Near the end of my writing, my dear friend Peggy Ostrem kindly helped me with proofing my work. I thank each and every one for their role in my story.

Throughout our married life, John and I have drawn little attention to our rather unique beginning. I'm proud of him for accepting
to expose our lives for anyone to view. There aren't many years left
for us here on this earth, so why not? Ours is a true love story. I thank
our daughter Rima for going over pages with a discerning eye. The
best part was she found hidden in my story the title for this book, My
Heart Is Singing! For truly, praise God, my heart is singing.

# ABOUT THE AUTHOR

Myrna Kinsinger Farraj worked as a longtime teacher and school counselor before publishing her writing debut, My Heart is Singing.

Myrna grew up in the Mennonite tradition while her husband of over fifty years, John, was raised Greek Orthodox. For many years they both have been members of St. Andrew Presbyterian Church in their hometown of Iowa City, Iowa.

The Palestinian cause remains a passion for Myrna, who continues to be active in interfaith peace efforts.

Myrna enjoys traveling, book club, bible study, volunteering, cooking Middle Eastern food, and entertaining friends and family from around the world alongside her husband. They have three children and six grandchildren.

Myrna can be reached at jamfarraj@icloud.com.